NEW ENGLAND
COAST GUARD
·STORIES·

Remarkable Mariners

DYKE HENDRICKSON

THE
History
PRESS

Published by The History Press
Charleston, SC
www.historypress.com

Front cover, top: Coast Guard members drill constantly on improving rescue techniques. *U.S. Coast Guard photo*; *bottom*: A Coast Guard vessel (*right*) is pictured with a rumrunning boat stopped during Prohibition times. *U.S. Coast Guard photo*.
Back cover, top: Helicopter pilot Jane Pena and others helped rescue crew of the sinking *Bounty* in the Atlantic in 2012. *Photo from collection of Jane Pena*; *bottom*: a Coast Guard vessel at the dock in Gloucester, Massachusetts. *Photo by Dyke Hendrickson*.

First published 2020

Manufactured in the United States

ISBN 9781467140041

Library of Congress Control Number: 2019954279

Contents

Acknowledgements 5

Introduction: Coast Guard Serves New England
  in Many Ways 7

New England Notes: Reflecting on Coast Guard
  People and Places 13

Tough Mission: All Hands on Deck: Admiral Dan May and
  the Search for JFK Jr. Off Massachusetts 23

MODERN COAST GUARD, PART I
SERVICE PREPARES TO DEFEND AGAINST AGGRESSORS
1. September 11 Attacks Changed New England,
  Led to Death of Connecticut Service Member 29
2. Rear Admiral Poulin Led New England with Authority,
  Goodwill 33
3. "Mustang" Paul Rooney Renders Service around the Country 37
4. Commander John Christensen Captains Cutter that
  Halts Drug Flow 40
5. From Minnesota to Middle East to New Hampshire 43

MODERN COAST GUARD, PART II
PRESENCE OF WOMEN HAS CHANGED FACE OF SERVICE
6. Captain Claudia Gelzer and the History of Women
  in Coast Guard 49
7. Only Woman at Maine Outpost 53
8. A View from Quiet, Coastal Jonesport, Maine 55

CONTENTS

9. A Commander in Connecticut: Valerie Boyd's Postings
Have Included New London, New Haven — 58
10. A Chief Boatswain's Mate Remembers a Rescue
Off Martha's Vineyard — 61

MODERN COAST GUARD, PART III
SERVICE ON SEA AND ON LAND
11. Heartland Native Remembers Assisting Plane, Vessel — 67
12. A Rescue Broken Off but Then a Fatal Moment
Near Gloucester — 70
13. Coast Guard's "Inland" Stations Include
Burlington, Vermont — 73
14. A Career on Land Reaching to South Portland, Maine — 75
15. Getting an Education, Running a Station in
New Hampshire — 78
16. Commanding Officer of Buoy Tender Operates
Out of Rhode Island — 81
17. A Surfman in Newburyport Remembers a Trainee
Flipping a Forty-Seven-Footer — 84
18. Commander Mixes Career and Family, from
New Orleans to Boston — 87
19. Master Chief Mentors in Connecticut — 90
20. Veteran in Maine Retells Family Story about Rescue at Sea
during Civil War — 93
21. Retired Captain Heads Alumni Association after Starting
Family in Connecticut — 98
22. Auxiliary, Typified by Joe Amore, Is a Powerful Force
that Supports Coast Guard — 101
23. New England Played Key Role in History of the
Coast Guard — 107
24. A Rumrunner, a Foggy Night and the Death of
a Coastie Off Massachusetts during Prohibition — 120
25. New England's Coast Guard Cities: Rockland,
Newburyport, New London — 128

Epilogue: Stations Have Closed but Coast Guard
in New England Stays Strong — 137
Bibliography — 141
About the Author — 143

Acknowledgements

I want to express my appreciation to numerous people who helped with the framing, research and writing of this book. Thanks to Beth Welch for proofreading.

Individuals who were hugely helpful were Coast Guard members who participated in many personal interviews. After Rear Admiral Steven Poulin himself sat for an interview—and endorsed the project—Coast Guard members of all stripes were informative and helpful. I want to thank Admiral Poulin in particular. He was the commanding officer of First Coast Guard District (New England). He gave a great interview and opened doors so I could identify many vibrant Coast Guard professionals.

Others who provided thoughtful suggestions included Captain Andrea Marcille (ret.), Commander Valerie Boyd, Master Chief Jay Galazin, retired enlistee Ralph Stevens and Auxiliary instructor Joe Amore.

Appreciation also is extended to Joan Whitlow, executive director of the Custom House Maritime Museum in Newburyport, and to Michael Mroz, who is the former director there. I am currently the outreach historian for that institution, which is working to expand the reach of local history. The team at the Custom House Maritime Museum in Newburyport has enabled me to carry out valuable research.

Librarians and museum directors were helpful as well, including those in Rockland, Maine; Portland, Maine; South Portland, Maine; Portsmouth, New Hampshire; Newburyport, Massachusetts; Gloucester, Massachusetts;

Barnstable, Massachusetts; New London, Connecticut; New Haven, Connecticut; and Burlington, Vermont.

Sharon Spieldenner, who heads the archive division at the Newburyport Public Library, identified valuable research materials.

Paul Roszkowski of the Coast Guard's media services team in Los Angeles provided important material and introductions.

Assistance in providing research and/or logistical support came from generous souls including Jim Connolly, Jack Pramberg, Doug Muir, Kevin MacDonald, Joe Callahan, Ghlee Woodworth, Marge Motes, Skip Motes, Stewart Lyttle and the late Bill Plante.

Dot Black in Rockland, Maine; Rear Admiral Daniel May (ret.) of Newburyport, Massachusetts; and Kat Wedge from Dracut, Massachusetts, were very helpful. I hope to write profiles of them in the future. Others providing valuable background include Mark Cutter, Rob Craighead and Ron Booth, all of the Newburyport area.

My cousin and longtime sailor Malcolm Powell, of Norwalk, Connecticut, offered useful suggestions. He also provided a spare bedroom when I was researching in Connecticut or New York.

One great thank-you goes to those who supported my Kickstarter campaign in the early winter of 2018. This is an online application that permits a writer or artist to generate funds for creative projects. I raised close to $5,000 from fifty contributors, and I couldn't have gotten a good start if I didn't have this early financial support for travel and research materials. One of my frustrations, however, is the Kickstarter application did not provide the names of all contributors. Many were listed as "anonymous." Thank you very much, even if I can't single you out by name!

Generous contributors include the following: Sadru and Clare Dunphy Hemani, Peter Wendell, Bob Connors, Dale Magee, Moss Quinlan, John Macone, Leslie Hendrickson, Drew Hendrickson, Natalia Martinez, Vicki Hendrickson, Wade Crowfoot, Dara Crowfoot, Jim Crowfoot, Josiah and Deirdre Welch, Andrew Mungo, Dr. Keith Ablow, Dr. Guy Navarra, Dr. Chad MacDonald, Paul Mills, Anne and Alec White, Tess Gerritsen, Jerry Lischke, Dr. Leif Bakland, Elizabeth Welch, Ron and Suzanne Rusay, Bob Richard, Brian Hotchkiss, Dr. Chandra Modi, Andre and Fontaine Dubus, Jacalyn Bennett, Geoff Nixon, Bruce Leonard, Ted Podkul, Rick Mesard, John Haass, Enzo DiMaio, Rob Mendel, John Burness and Dan Wagner.

Introduction

COAST GUARD SERVES NEW ENGLAND IN MANY WAYS

The U.S. Coast Guard is one of this country's great waterborne assets. Coasties do much, and they are always there even if they do seem to function in the public shadow of the other armed services. The Coast Guard saves lives, patrols waterways, protects the marine environment, responds to natural disasters and much more.

Books have been written about the Coast Guard as an institution. But there have been few texts that provide profiles of those in uniform. In this book, members of the "fifth service" speak. Also, the history of the service is reviewed, with emphasis on what has happened in New England. The intent is to focus light on a service that does much and asks little in return.

The Coast Guard was founded in Newburyport, Massachusetts, in 1790, though the service was not known by that name until 1915. It has been known by several names, including the Revenue Marine and Revenue Cutter Service.

Much of its early history revolves around the six northeastern states, from northern Maine to southern Connecticut. The first of the service's revenue cutters, the *Massachusetts*, was launched in that state in 1791.

The Life-Saving Service also has its roots in New England states, where many hearty lifesavers heeded the call, "You have to go out but you don't have to come back." The Life-Saving Service and the Revenue Cutter Service were merged in 1915 to create the U.S. Coast Guard. The Lighthouse Service was melded into this organization in 1939 to form the modern Coast Guard as we know it.

This text provides profiles of those who have served here and explains the valuable work that they do. One important caveat must guide the reader: service members are transferred with regularity. An individual featured in *New England Coast Guard Stories* might be an officer or enlisted person who is no longer in the region. That means that a Boston-based admiral, such as Rear Admiral Steven Poulin, might have been interviewed in 2018, but he could be serving in Miami when you read this book. That is the case. Or master petty officer Lori Fields might have been in South Portland, Maine, and now finds herself in Hawaii. Yet everyone depicted here has a connection to New England. The goal is to convey the spirit and tone of the Coast Guard in the region.

The stations in the six New England states are part of the First Coast Guard District: New England, New York and northern New Jersey. This book focuses on New England, where many veterans are known as members of the "D-1 Mafia." This refers to those who choose—or maneuver—to serve hitches at stations in New England.

In addition, *New England Coast Guard Stories* notes major changes in the modern Coast Guard.

One occurred on September 11, 2001, when terrorist attacks killed Americans—and sounded the alarm in all branches of the military. Most veterans in New England remember where they were when the attacks were announced.

The Coast Guard was soon given much more responsibility, and its role as a waterfront watchdog was greatly increased. Federal officials transferred the Coast Guard from the Transportation Department to the Department of Homeland Security, and the service developed a more military posture. Personal profiles reflect the effect that the attacks had on individuals.

The second section of the book looks at another major change: the growing number of female officers and enlisted personnel. The Coast Guard Academy in New London, Connecticut, began accepting women in 1976. The first females graduated from the Coast Guard Academy in 1980. Most Coast Guard officials feel that the presence of women (15 to 20 percent today) has been an asset, and numerous profiles of female service members are included here. Efforts were made to include as many profiles of women as of men.

If there is one characteristic that links many active members of the Coast Guard, it is the desire to help. Almost every Coast Guard regular I interviewed said a key reason for joining was the desire to help others.

The use of helicopters, which were developed in Connecticut, has enabled the service to make lifesaving rescues at sea. *U.S. Coast Guard photo.*

The Coast Guard takes its change-of-command ceremonies seriously. Here, top officers gathered at Faneuil Hall in Boston to bid farewell to Rear Admiral Steven D. Poulin (*right*) and welcome Rear Admiral Andrew J. Tiongson (*left*) as commander of the First District. Vice Admiral Scott A. Buschman, commander, Coast Guard Atlantic Area (*center*), presided over the ceremony. *U.S. Coast Guard photo by Petty Officer Amber Howie.*

Lighthouses are nostalgic icons that have helped many mariners. The U.S. Lighthouse Service became part of the Coast Guard in 1939. Here is Portland Head Light, Cape Elizabeth, Maine. *U.S. Coast Guard photo by Ayla Kelley.*

Without exception, those I interviewed said that a major reward of the job is that they saved a boat or helped bring injured mariners to safety.

Most have been in harm's way. Officers talk of boarding drug-running vessels and not knowing if those aboard will emerge armed and shooting. And some crews have been ordered into danger without knowing if they would come back alive.

Several crews flew into Superstorm Sandy in 2012 to rescue members of the tall ship *Bounty*, which had sailed from New London, Connecticut, just days before. In heavy winds and roiling seas, choppers sped seventy miles into the Atlantic and saved fourteen of sixteen crew members. Those who thrive in the Coast Guard are a special breed. They are thoughtful, responsible and inclined to help others.

Not everyone is cut out to serve in the Coast Guard. Some don't want the discipline and responsibility that the jobs entail. But those who stay in the service seem to love it. Many remain in for twenty years or more, and if they leave then, they are young enough to start a second career.

On a related point, the Coast Guard is a great resource for young men and women who do not know exactly what they want to do with their lives. Many I interviewed said they had been aimless and unsure of their future until

Rescue by powerful helicopters has been a crucial mission in the modern era. *U.S. Coast Guard photo.*

they joined the Coast Guard. The service provides order and discipline. And if they succeed, the service will pay for them to finish college. Those with college degrees often earn a master's degree at the expense of the service. The Coast Guard Academy is the only military service academy to which candidates don't need a congressional appointment to be accepted.

Those in the Coast Guard are in a position to help on sea or on land. One officer depicted here left the Navy after three years so he would have more to do and so he could "be of service every day."

That is what this book is about—women and men who are of service every day. We should feel fortunate that we have them out there.

REFLECTING ON COAST GUARD PEOPLE AND PLACES

The story goes that when President George Washington gave approval to Treasury secretary Alexander Hamilton in 1789 to start a revenue cutter service—later the Coast Guard—he told Hamilton to urge members of the new service to be cordial, firm and efficient.

"Many captains and crew members have just come from the Revolutionary War," Washington is reputed to have said. "They are tough, experienced sailors and they won't want to be pushed around." He seemed to be saying "Don't be rude" and "Show respect for fellow seamen."

This admonition appears to have carried over more than two centuries, for those whom I met from northern Maine to southern Connecticut during my research were polite but always competent and in control. I conducted interviews at more than a dozen New England stations. Once I explained what I was doing, everyone extended cooperation.

But Semper Paratus—Always Ready. I obtained cooperation by contacting the national Coast Guard office of media, print and film in Los Angeles. After I sent officers a copy of my publishing contract with The History Press, I obtained approval to talk with both officers and enlisted personnel.

And then I got an interview with Admiral Steven Poulin, the commanding officer for all New England operations. Facilitating that interview was Lieutenant Karen Love Kutkiewicz, a public information aide in his office. His office was in Boston, and he had eleven thousand personnel under his command when counting actives, reserves, auxiliary members and civilian

A Coast Guard vessel is berthed near lobster pots in Gloucester, Massachusetts. Coast Guard personnel have always interacted with fishermen. *Dyke Hendrickson photo.*

employees. We spoke for about an hour. Poulin, born in Kittery, Maine, liked the idea of a book and later sent a letter of endorsement.

Thereafter, I often let it be known to interviewees that I had recently interviewed *the admiral*. As most service personnel know, it can help to mention the name of a superior officer. And since there are only about forty-two admirals in the forty-two-thousand-member Coast Guard, the invocation of the name of Admiral Poulin added to my credibility—and resulted in better interviews.

I visited Rockland, Maine, on numerous occasions. There I interviewed Meghan Cahoon, who went to Ohio Wesleyan University before enlisting. She has roots in Rockport, Maine, and Montpelier, Vermont, and she said that Rockland was a great posting.

In Rockland, I had an enlightening interview with Paul Dilger. He is a native of North Dakota who spent thirty years in the Coast Guard. He had been posted in Rockland on the *Abby Burgess*. He retired in Rockland, where he is the chairman of the board of the Maine Lighthouse Museum. The museum was pioneered by Ken Black, a career service member who died in 2006. His widow, Dot Black, runs the venue now. She was a key force in Rockland being designated a Coast Guard city in 2008. She invited me

Women have changed the face of the Coast Guard, as this image from the Coast Guard Academy in New London, Connecticut, suggests. Women first entered the Academy in 1976. *U.S. Coast Guard photo*.

Coast Guard cadets come to attention during drills at the Coast Guard Academy. This institution is the one military academy that does not require congressional appointments. *U.S. Coast Guard photo*.

to speak there in October 2018. It's a great museum, with Coast Guard memorabilia as well as that relating to the Lighthouse Service.

One of the great wonders of New England is the breakwater and lighthouse in Rockland Harbor. The sturdy stone wall extends seven-eighths of a mile, though it does not appear that long when one begins walking. Most turn back.

Rockland hosts a major transportation center for ferries going to islands including Vinalhaven and Matinicus. Ensuring safety of vessels and passengers is another reason why the Coast Guard is a valued asset on Penobscot Bay.

Farther south in Boothbay Harbor lives Mark Colby, who was a Coast Guard radioman in the early '80s. He left the service after about four years and went on to teach school and to captain private vessels. Until recently, he captained a craft that took tourists into the Atlantic to witness the clever antics of the ever-cute puffins.

Colby comes from a long stock of blue-water captains, many of whom sailed two centuries ago out of Newburyport, Massachusetts. He mentioned a seagoing circumstance of which I was not aware. During the Civil War, Confederate ships traveling in waters halfway around the world boarded and burned Yankee vessels that had nothing to do with the war. One of his distant relatives was almost killed near Calcutta by the Confederate vessel *Alabama* in about 1863. I have used that anecdote in a profile of him.

Boothbay Harbor is also the community at which the tall ship *Bounty* was refitted in 2012. The vessel, captained by Robin Walbridge, a native of Montpelier, Vermont, sailed from New London, Connecticut, in October

Lieutenant Commander Rob Craighead had his retirement party at the Custom House Maritime Museum in Newburyport, Massachusetts. *Dyke Hendrickson photo.*

2012 toward a business engagement in Florida. It foolishly strayed into Hurricane Sandy. Walbridge, instead of heading for a port, chose to sail east, ostensibly to get out of the way of the storm. Sandy was huge, and Coast Guard critical reports later declared the vessel should have stayed in port rather than venture out into a storm that spread across the south Atlantic.

The vessel's pumps failed, and it lost power. Crew members (but not Walbridge) issued a panicky call to the Coast Guard for immediate help. In churning seas and howling winds, a Coast Guard fixed-wing aircraft located the foundering vessel about seventy miles off North Carolina. The Coast Guard launched one of its most amazing helicopter rescues ever, dropping rescue swimmers into the savage sea to save fourteen of sixteen crew members. Walbridge and amateur crew member Claudene Christian did not survive. She was a distant relative of Fletcher Christian,

legendary figure of the old HMS *Bounty* in the well-known story *Mutiny on the Bounty*. Claudene was located but did not live; Walbridge was never found. Still, saving fourteen of sixteen crew members in a howling hurricane was a major achievement of a courageous Coast Guard crew.

In 2018, I interviewed Lieutenant Jane Pena, a copilot of one of the helicopters involved in the harrowing rescue. She said her crew got orders at 5:00 a.m. She explained, "We went online to see what the ship looked like. I hadn't heard of it and didn't think any ships could be at sea in this storm. There had been plenty of warning that Sandy covered a huge amount of ocean."

Pena declined to speculate on the captain's choices. "I wouldn't want to comment on any decisions made because it might sound like I was talking for the Coast Guard. I will say I am glad we were trained and ready for a tough assignment. I am thankful we recovered so many and that our crew returned safely."

Jane Pena is a helicopter copilot, and one of her most challenging rescues involved saving fourteen crew members of the tall ship *Bounty*, which sank in 2012 after sailing from Connecticut. It got caught in Hurricane Sandy. *Photo from collection of Jane Pena.*

The officer added, "In the Coast Guard, there is a lot of attention to preparation. The service gives you the tools to succeed."

One of the service's major stations is in South Portland, Maine. The Coast Guard also maintains offices in Portland, the larger municipality across Casco Bay. I always feel comfortable returning to Portland because I was a writer and editor on the *Portland Press Herald* for more than a decade. Since the Coast Guard was transferred to the Department of Homeland Security after the attacks of September 11, 2001, the service has been tasked with a larger array of security duties.

For instance, Portland is one of the largest ports on the East Coast for offloading oil. Product coming into the harbor is transferred to a pipeline running to Montreal. The Coast Guard must ensure safety of arriving vessels. The port still hosts scores of working fishing and lobstering boats, and Coasties inspect them for fitness, as well as come to their aid if they founder.

My interview with Command Master Chief Lori Fields in South Portland amplified the notion that not everyone makes their careers by going out to sea. Quicker advancement and better placements come as a result of sea duty. But Fields said that her career has been mostly on land.

Recruited in 1992, Fields got married in 1994 to SK1 Chuck Fields, USCG (ret.), and they have a son, Spencer. She indicated that an administrative career would make it easier for them to develop a family. Marriage is a commonplace occurrence among service types, and current members say the service has been accommodating in recent years in helping spouses be assigned together.

Much of her work has been involved with pay and personnel issues. In her posting at South Portland, she was an advisor to sector commanders on policies relating to families in Maine, New Hampshire and Vermont. She has had close to a dozen postings in her stellar career, mostly on land.

Many people don't know that the Coast Guard maintains many inland stations, including one in Burlington, Vermont. I traveled there in the spring of 2018 and met with two enlisted personnel, Chris Batton and Jason Balmer.

The station is on Lake Champlain. Because it is adjacent to the Canadian border, they are alert for illegal immigration and drug importation. And when the snow melts, they have several vessels ready for search-and-rescue missions. Actually, search and rescue can take place in winter as well. For reasons I have never been able to understand, good ol' boys in New England often drive their pickup trucks onto nearby lakes for some fishing. Sometimes the vehicles go through the ice. Indeed, one of the Burlington station's regular practice routines is making rescues on the ice.

Above: The Coast Guard station in Burlington, Vermont, is on Lake Champlain. *Dyke Hendrickson photo.*

Left: This well-known statue in Gloucester suggests that many skippers have been challenged by the Atlantic. *Dyke Hendrickson photo.*

In Portsmouth, New Hampshire, I met one of the most well-traveled members in the group in New England: Amanda Fenstermacher. She had served in Alaska and Virginia. And because she trained as an international security expert, she traveled to close to a dozen foreign lands. Her postings have included Brazil, where she helped train security teams prior to the Olympics and World Cup in 2016. She has also served in Djibouti, Haiti, Italy, Mexico, Peru and Uganda, teaching courses including Port and Waterway Coast Security.

The officer in charge at Portsmouth was Chief Petty Officer John Harker, who has taken advantage of Coast Guard education supplements to get a bachelor's degree. He is working on a master's degree in national security.

After talking with service members like Harker, one of my takeaways is that the Coast Guard is an excellent landing spot for those who have not finished college. Some enlistees weren't ready for four-year college. Others didn't want the expense—and subsequent debt. Harker has advanced his education in the service. The Coast Guard has helped thousands in pursing education goals with minimum expense.

In Massachusetts, one of my most intriguing interviews was with Ralph Stevens, who served from 1974 to 1978. He was assigned to the station in Gloucester when the Blizzard of '78 came barreling through. A large tanker was foundering off Gloucester, and off-site officers ordered a forty-one-footer to launch. Visibility was zero. Off-site officers called off the search. But Stevens recalled that a pilot boat nearby, the *Can Do*, left the harbor in an effort to help the vessel. The fifty-foot craft was lost with five good Samaritans aboard. All died in the incident.

Also in Gloucester, I met with Chief Boatswain's Mate J. Chris Lobherr. He has an interest in oceanography, and he reminded me that the Coast Guard is a major player in scientific research with other federal agencies, including the National Science Foundation and the National Oceanographic and Atmospheric Administration.

There's no longer much Coast Guard activity in nearby Salem, Massachusetts. With the advent of fast-moving helicopters, which were pioneered by Igor Sikorsky of Connecticut in the 1930s and '40s, the air station in Salem went dark. Now, aircraft respond to emergencies from Woods Hole, Massachusetts.

In Boston, Rear Admiral Steven Poulin stressed the need for individual safety, especially on personal "vessels" such as kayaks, surfboards and paddle boards.

Also in Boston was Commander John Christensen, who is the commanding officer of the 270-foot *Seneca*. I met him at the reception when Admiral Poulin was replaced by Rear Admiral Andrew Tiongson. Christensen had been in the Navy for three years but transferred to the Coast Guard so he would have more to do. He indicated that the Navy doesn't offer much activity in peace time.

The *Seneca* and a similar Boston-based cutter, the *Escanaba*, are frequently assigned to the Caribbean. They routinely confiscate thousands of pounds of illegal drugs. I once posted on Facebook an item about the good work they are doing in stopping the arrival of cocaine, and I got hundreds of "likes" and "shares." Those who commented said they are very proud of these patriots who patrol the seas.

Officers on such vessels also are tasked with halting unsound vessels from traveling to the United States from Haiti or the Dominican Republic. They say they are actually saving lives, since many vessels are poorly constructed and frequently sink during rough weather.

In Rhode Island, I met with Commander Greg Batchelder, commanding officer of the buoy tender *Juniper*. The Coast Guard station is on the grounds of the large naval deployment there, and security was tight. Indeed, it took me ninety minutes to traverse a half mile (and four sentry posts) on Navy grounds even though I had a pass. I am glad I visited a buoy tender so I could learn firsthand what an important role they play in keeping channels and harbors equipped with navigation aids. The vast majority of American trade is transported via waterways, and buoys and lighthouses are keys to safety and security.

Commander Valerie Boyd was one of numerous officers I met in Connecticut. She has risen steadily in the Coast Guard and has earned many awards and citations. One question I ask at an interview is, "Is there

Vice Admiral Vivien Crea, now retired, was the first woman to hold flag rank in the Coast Guard. *U.S. Coast Guard photo.*

anything that I didn't ask, or is there something you would like to mention to provide useful information for readers?"

"Well," the Coast Guard Academy graduate said modestly, "in the last ten years, in addition to my assignments, I've had three children who are doing great."

Good point. The Coast Guard in recent years has developed programs that help Coast Guard families with their domestic arrangements. It is also one of the leaders of the five military services in developing programs that outlaw harassment and inappropriate sexual behavior.

In New London, I had an informative interview with Boatswain's Master Mate Jay Galazin, who joined the Coast Guard at twenty-seven— the maximum age of enlistment. He has had a remarkable career and has been assigned to train others at the Coast Guard Academy in that community.

In Norwalk, Connecticut, I encountered a distinguished civilian, my cousin Malcolm Powell. He is retired from a successful career in nuclear medicine in New York City and Norwalk, and he invited me to stay with him during my interview trips to that state. He is a great sailing enthusiast who once called on the Coast Guard for aid. During an unexpected storm on a return trip from Bermuda to New England in the mid-'80s, his vessel lost a rudder. And the pumps weren't working too well, either. The small crew was able to contact the Coast Guard, which was able to drop a pumping device. An extra rudder was found. And cousin Malcolm emerged happy, healthy and with great appreciation for the Coasties who provided aid.

How's that for a consumer endorsement?

Tough Mission

ALL HANDS ON DECK: ADMIRAL DAN MAY AND THE SEARCH FOR JFK JR. OFF MASSACHUSETTS

On the evening of July 16, 1999, the small private plane piloted by John F. Kennedy Jr. was reported missing off Martha's Vineyard off the coast of Massachusetts. The son of the late president was traveling with his wife, Carolyn Bessette, and his sister-in-law, Lauren Bessette.

The aircraft had departed a New Jersey airport at 8:40 p.m. At 2:15 a.m., the Kennedy family, on nearby Cape Cod for a family wedding, reported to the Coast Guard that the plane had not arrived.

Rear Admiral (ret.) Daniel May was then a commander. He was chosen to serve as operations division chief for the JFK assignment. He was a key leader in the frantic effort to find the plane and its passengers—hopefully still alive. The operation proved to be one of the most intricate of his career.

The response of May and his team might qualify under the service's mantra: Semper Paratus, Always Ready. With no advance notice, units were scrambled to search for the aircraft.

May was an engineer, and he served as industrial manager of the Coast Guard Integrated Support Command in Boston. In those early morning hours two decades ago, his team started out as a rescue unit and emerged as a recovery team.

It was later determined that the Piper Saratoga light aircraft crashed nose-first at about 9:41 p.m. But May and his team didn't know this at that time.

May, who has retired in Newburyport, Massachusetts, said the operation was complex and involved hundreds of Coast Guard personnel.

"The search for JFK's plane started as a search for the proverbial needle in a haystack," recalled May in an interview. "We didn't have much to go on initially, and in true Coast Guard fashion, we sent all assets that we had available, including boats, helicopters and planes.

"We had support from other agencies like the Massachusetts State Police marine unit and the Environmental Police marine units. As we gathered more information on the flight path and discovered a few small pieces of debris had washed up on Martha's Vineyard, we began to narrow the search area.

"We found wreckage of a plane, and word went out that the chances of finding survivors was small."

The search was extensive. President Bill Clinton said at the time, "If anyone believes that a lengthy search was wrong, the Coast Guard is not at fault—I am. It was because I thought it was the right thing to do under the circumstances."

May recalled, "It was a daunting task. With no success of finding anything on the surface, we next obtained the support of two NOAA [National Atmospheric and Oceanographic Administration] ships that were equipped with side-scan sonar and began a round-the-clock underwater search.

"The Navy also joined in with several other ships which included underwater dive teams. For the next two days, I, along with two other officers and an expert trained in underwater sonar recovery, pored over side-scan sonar plots as they came into the command center.

"We then made an all-out search over the area with our NOAA ships. I distinctly remember staring at a plot when the underwater search expert was sitting next to me and said, 'There's your plane.'

"We then directed the Navy planes over the location, and they deployed a small remote-operated vehicle with a remote video camera. Sure enough, there was the plane. Then we began the intricate recovery of the victims and the plane."

There are about four dozen admirals in the Coast Guard at a given time, and the activities that May directed over his career suggest he was one of the most versatile of the top brass. He was an engineer engaged in nautical issues and served for more than three decades near the water.

A native of Florida, he considered attending the Naval Academy and the Coast Guard Academy. He opted for the Coast Guard Academy and graduated in 1979 after majoring in ocean engineering. He earned a master's degree in ocean engineering at the University of Rhode Island in 1984.

"When I was making decisions years ago," said May, who is now the director of the Regional Municipal Police Academy in Reading, Massachusetts, "I realized the Coast Guard was the place for me. I loved the idea of each day being an opportunity to save a life, helping someone in need or to protect our country from harm."

When he was chief of the design team for the U.S. Coast Guard Civil Engineering Unit in Providence, Rhode Island, he designed more than fifty major lighthouse projects throughout the region. In one of his most complicated assignments, he was supervisor of the initiative to relocate and renovate the Block Island (Rhode Island) Lighthouse, the first major lighthouse structure to be moved by the Coast Guard. In an era in which lighthouses were under duress from both erosion and age, May played a significant role in preserving the popular nautical icons.

One of his high-visibility roles was working with Senator Ted Kennedy to change the staffing and develop renovations at Boston Light in that city's harbor.

The affable admiral said, "I never dreamed I would serve nearly thirty-four years on active duty and reach the rank of rear admiral; I just enjoyed

Rear Admiral Daniel May (ret.) was a commander when he led a team seeking the Kennedy plane. The bodies of Kennedy; his wife, Caroline Bessette Kennedy; and her sister, Lauren Bessette, were recovered after a lengthy search. *U.S. Coast Guard photo.*

each day as it came and tried to do my very best to serve my country and all those men and women that worked with me.

"I count myself as being truly blessed with every assignment I had; my greatest satisfaction was in the many engineering lighthouse projects completed and in those actions that directly affected people's lives."

May, who is often called to host Coast Guard ceremonial events throughout New England, earned numerous awards during his career. He received three Legion of Merit Awards, two commendation medals, four Coast Guard Commendation medals, three Achievement Medals, three Special Operation Awards, two Unit Commendation Awards and three Meritorious Unit Commendations.

Also, he received the 2011 Reserve Officer Association Minuteman Hall of Fame Award and the University of Rhode Island Distinguished Alumni Award (2012). He is the recipient of the Oren Medal for most significant contributions to Coast Guard Civil Engineering (1992).

Senior leadership positions he held included assistant superintendent of the Coast Guard Academy (2006–8). Also, he was commander of the Coast Guard Personnel Service Center in charge of all human resource functions including recruiting, assignment, advancement and promotion for the Coast Guard's workforce of fifty thousand, including all active and reserve personnel (2010–12).

· MODERN COAST GUARD, PART I ·

SERVICE PREPARES TO DEFEND AGAINST AGGRESSORS

Chapter 1

SEPTEMBER 11 ATTACKS CHANGED NEW ENGLAND, LED TO DEATH OF CONNECTICUT SERVICE MEMBER

T he Coast Guard in New England was greatly affected by the terrorist attacks of September 11, 2001. And strife in the Middle East indirectly led to the death of a petty officer with roots in Connecticut.

The First Coast Guard District headquarters is in Boston. When the first news of the attacks flashed, Coast Guard officers and enlisted personnel throughout New England rushed into action. Hundreds in uniform saved thousands of civilians in the Atlantic sector, as the Coast Guard joined other first responders in reacting to the unexpected tragedy in New York City. Thousands were evacuated by Coast Guard boats and other vessels near the Battery in New York, and some historians have called the evacuation "another Dunkirk."

Coast Guard units also moved quickly to secure other ports in New England. Not much was known in the early hours after the attack, and every unit was put on alert.

It's likely that Coast Guard veterans remember where they were on that sunny morning. Indeed, the shocking call-to-action event might stand for this generation as did the Pearl Harbor attack in the early '40s and the slaying of President Kennedy in the '60s.

The responsibilities of the Coast Guard were expanded following this incident. Dr. William Thiesen, Coast Guard historian for the Atlantic region, wrote, "The 2001 terrorist attacks reshaped the Coast Guard, including new homeland security units, alterations in existing Coast Guard units and the transition to a new federal agency (Homeland Security). The service's response represented the greatest transformation since World War II."

Rear Admiral Steven Poulin, who was the commanding officer of New England operations in Boston from 2016 to 2018, said, "The attacks resulted in more responsibility for the Coast Guard. There was more boarding of international vessels and added responsibility for escorting commercial and government ships into port.

"We were suddenly more alert and now planned every action with security in mind."

Retired Petty Officer Paul Dilger, now of Rockland, Maine, said his ship was in the Pacific when the attacks occurred. He recalled, "Security became essential everywhere, and the Coast Guard seemed to have more standing after we were transferred to the Department of Homeland Security.

"Before that, we were on a very low tier when it came to funding. After the attacks, Congress had security in mind, and we got more funding and greater resources."

Near Boston, for instance, Coast Guard vessels with blue lights flashing escorted liquid nitrogen tankers to their berths in Chelsea. In Portland, Maine, and Portsmouth, New Hampshire, Coast Guard vessels accompanied fuel tankers and cargo carriers into port.

Historians say that in late 2001, President George W. Bush made formal plans for greater security. In November 2002, he signed the Homeland Security Act creating the Department of Homeland Security (DHS). By March 2003, the Coast Guard had been transferred from the Department of Transportation to Homeland Security and suddenly became the largest agency within DHS.

Coast Guard Intelligence became part of the nation's intelligence community.

President Bush also signed the Maritime Transportation Security Act (MTSA) to protect the nation's ports and waterways from terrorist attacks. Historians say the MTSA led indirectly to the International Ship and Port Facility Code and the formation of an International Port Security Program whose members monitor security standards in foreign ports.

At least one Coast Guard death was indirectly tied to strife fostered by those in the Middle East. Residents of the small Connecticut town of Ridgefield mourned the death in a war zone in 2004 of the first member of the Coast Guard to die in action since the Vietnam War. Damage Controlman Third Class Nathan B. Bruckenthal was killed in a weekend attack at an Iraqi oil terminal.

Bruckenthal attended Ridgefield High School and was a volunteer firefighter for the town when he was a teenager. "He would come to almost all the [fire] calls he could," Michael Gabbianelli, a friend and fellow firefighter, said in 2004. "He was always there to help people."

Bruckenthal, twenty-four, was a damage controlman originally from Smithtown, New York. He died of wounds after suicide bombers attacked pumping stations in the Persian Gulf. Terrorists' boats exploded as they were approached by U.S. military teams. Two Navy sailors also were killed in the attack.

Bruckenthal played football for Ridgefield High School and was involved with a club that helped students who were new to the school, said educator Linda Jaslow in 2004. She was Bruckenthal's high school guidance teacher.

He often spoke of wanting to be a police officer or firefighter, she said. "He was so friendly and outgoing. He was just a really, really nice kid." Bruckenthal left Ridgefield midway through high school when his parents moved, but friends say he continued to return to the community. "He was always around. It felt like he never left," said Gabbianelli.

"He would come up for weekends and in the summer, and we had a good time." They would play pool and listen to music together, he said.

This plaque memorializes the loss of Coast Guard Petty Officer Third Class Nathan B. Bruckenthal. He was killed near Iraq; he had roots in Connecticut. *U.S. Coast Guard photo by Seaman Jourdin M. Pitts.*

When the incident occurred, Bruckenthal was scheduled to return within a month from his second stint in Iraq, Commander Glenn Grahl said in 2004.

Ridgefield first selectman Rudy Marconi said at the time that Bruckenthal's death was a loss that would be felt by the Ridgefield community and throughout the country. "It makes you give more serious thought to why we are there," he said. "When you see a young life like this lost in a war that is questionable, it makes it very difficult for everyone."

The Coast Guard has participated in all U.S. wars, including ongoing conflicts in the Middle East.

Part of this story originated with the Associated Press in 2004.

Chapter 2

REAR ADMIRAL POULIN LED NEW ENGLAND WITH AUTHORITY, GOODWILL

When Rear Admiral Steven Poulin reflects on the changing role of the Coast Guard, he sometimes mentions that it has become a very valuable force in commerce throughout the country. "The Coast Guard is in charge of port and waterway security," said Poulin. "About 90 percent of this country's trade comes on the waterways. We keep America open for business."

Poulin, who was the commanding officer of the New England sector from 2016 to 2018, knows about the changing and increasing role the service has had. He has been in the Coast Guard for almost four decades, after graduating from the U.S. Coast Guard Academy in New London, Connecticut.

His tenure includes one of the most momentous security events in American history: the terrorist attacks of September 11, 2001. Since that day, Americans have had a greater focus on maritime and port security. Indeed, Coasties board vessels every day in ports serving oceans, rivers and lakes.

"We have regulatory power now, and we are responsible for safety and security measures," said Poulin, who had eleven thousand people answering to him when he headed the First Coast Guard District. "We've improved our readiness and have built a greater capacity to patrol and react. We are responsible for a great many missions."

Indeed, the official manifesto of the service includes the following responsibilities: port and water security, drug interdiction, aids to navigation,

Rear Admiral Steven Poulin, then First Coast Guard District (New England) commander, *center*, and Captain Michael Baroody, then commander of Coast Guard Sector Northern New England, *left*, speak with Edward Fish, Pease Air National Guard Base Air Traffic Control manager, *right*, during their visit to Pease Air National Guard Base in New Hampshire. *Air National Guard photo by Master Sergeant Thomas Johnson.*

search and rescue, preserving marine resources, marine safety, defense readiness, migrant interdiction, marine environmental protection, ice-breaking operations and law enforcement.

To head an organization with missions of such gravitas, a leader must be prepared. When leading the First District, Poulin supervised on organization that utilized two hundred boats, thirty cutters and seven aircraft.

Poulin appears qualified. He has a law degree from University of Miami Law School and master's degrees from George Washington University (environmental law), the U.S. Army War College (strategic studies) and the University of South Alabama (public administration).

Poulin can also be a capable advisor. "He was a good mentor to me," said Captain Claudia Gelzer, who served in the Boston headquarters at the same time. "He was very helpful when I talked with him, especially about my thoughts for the future."

Poulin's many missions have included as chief counsel of the Coast Guard; director of social engagement with Congress and the media; and as chief of the Office of Maritime and International Law. He served as commander of

Coast Guard Sector Mobile, Alabama, and was incident commander for the Deepwater Horizon oil spill.

While serving in Boston, Poulin said in an interview, "One Coast Guard goal is to educate the public on the problems on the water and raise public interest in our mission. If all Americans have a better understanding of the mission and value of the Coast Guard, there will be greater support from our work." The rear admiral indicated that political support from non-coastal states is important when Congress appropriates money or considers supporting its initiatives.

Poulin, whose father was in the Air Force, grew up near an Air Force base in Plattsburg, New York. He played football (running back) at the Coast Guard Academy, which he attended in part for his interest in contributing to the public good through search and rescue. During his decorated career, he said key advancements include the digitalization of Coast Guard functions and records. Also, the fleet in the twenty-first century has been upgraded with modern technology and weaponry to carry out its tasks.

Initiatives of his while in New England included working with the commercial fishing fleet to make its boats safer—and to avoid the ever-growing presence of opioids. He said, "We stress safety with commercial fishing captains, and we board their boats to make them safer. As part of our law enforcement responsibility, we work with fishing crews to know and avoid the dangers of opioid abuse on the water."

During his tenure in New England, his team stressed a program to encourage use of life jackets not only in pleasure boats but also when on kayaks and paddle boards. "People love to be on the water, but unexpected things can happen," he said. "In 2016–17, we saw a decrease of 11 percent of deaths on the water related to canoes, kayaks and paddle boards. In cold New England water, hypothermia can be a big factor. If you go in the water, you might not be able to paddle. We stress the use of life jackets for every water sport."

Poulin was promoted in June 2018 to a Coast Guard administrative office in Miami, where he assumed a top leadership role in the military administration of the Southern Hemisphere. Those attending his change of command ceremony in Boston's Faneuil Hall in June 2018 included family; friends; colleagues; city, state and federal leaders; and many members of his past and present Coast Guard staffs.

The affable Poulin was generous in his praise of those with whom he worked, from senior staff to newcomers. Perhaps reflecting his appreciation of everyone on the team, he praised his personal driver for constant and meritorious work. "I had been chosen to throw the first ball out at a Red Sox game," said Poulin. "I hadn't thrown a ball in years, and my driver was good enough to throw a ball with me [for weeks] before the game. I thank him—and everyone with whom I've worked—for making my time in New England memorable."

Chapter 3

"MUSTANG" PAUL ROONEY RENDERS SERVICE AROUND THE COUNTRY

P aul Rooney might be called a man for all seasons when it comes to maritime activities. He is a commander in the Coast Guard Reserve and frequently flies across the country when the service provides aid to residents threatened by hurricanes and subsequent flooding. His "day job" is as a federal officer with the U.S. Customs and Border Protection, assigned to the Boston field office. He supervises ports in Maine and New Hampshire.

And Rooney has become a part owner of Bob Lobster, a popular eatery on the Plum Island Turnpike near Newburyport, Massachusetts. Many visitors find a trip to the barrier island is not complete without a visit to the informal seafood restaurant.

Rooney is a native of Scituate, Massachusetts, whose father and grandfather both were in the Coast Guard. He joined in 1986 and was on active duty until 1992. He proved to be a natural and was chosen for Officer Candidate School (OCS), from which he graduated. He is what's called a "mustang," a serviceman who joined as an enlisted man and rose to become an officer. Coast Guard veterans say this is an admirable achievement.

After active service, he entered the Coast Guard Reserve and has been deployed to some of the greatest catastrophes of this century, including the 9/11 attack, Hurricane Katrina and Hurricane Sandy. He declined to make comparisons. "One was a terrorist attack, and others were natural disasters," he said. "Support was needed at all sites."

Paul Rooney is a commander in the Coast Guard Reserve and often is assigned to support missions providing relief after hurricanes. *Photo by Bryan Eaton, courtesy of the* Daily News, *Newburyport.*

In recent years, he has flown to Houston and Miami (the latter for Hurricane Maria, which affected Puerto Rico in 2017) to help residents and first responders react to these natural disasters. The Coast Guard does as much as it can to support the Federal Emergency Management Agency (FEMA) during cleanup operations.

After being assigned to travel to Houston a couple years ago, he said, "I didn't know where I'd be sleeping Friday night. I'd be there a minimum of thirty days and a maximum of sixty days. My assignment is to go and be part of the team providing support for the agencies and the people."

Rooney, a Newburyport-area resident, often serves as an emergency preparedness liaison officer between the Coast Guard and FEMA. For instance, if a FEMA executive had a sudden need for Coast Guard helicopters for rescue operations north of Houston, he would confer with Rooney.

Rooney would check local resources and likely contact top Coast Guard officers in Washington, D.C., or Boston to determine availability in other parts of the country. He would then tell FEMA what was available and when choppers could be deployed. In recent years, he has been the "admiral's representative" of the First District of the Coast Guard, which runs from northern New Jersey to Maine. The commanding officer for the district in 2018 was Rear Admiral Andrew J. Tiongson, based in Boston.

With two youngsters in school, Rooney enjoys getting home when missions are complete. Spending weeks in hurricane-torn areas can be hectic and tiring. But Rooney, once an Eagle Scout, said, "It's a challenge but one that I am willing to accept."

Chapter 4

COMMANDER JOHN CHRISTENSEN CAPTAINS CUTTER THAT HALTS DRUG FLOW

C
ommander John Christensen spent three years in the Navy before switching to the Coast Guard.

"I wanted a closer connection with people," said Christensen, who is commanding officer of the cutter *Seneca* (CG vessel 906). "In the Navy, there's a lot of routine drilling and not much to do when not in war. The Coast Guard has many missions, and we're all over the world. I like the opportunity of helping people."

The *Seneca* is a medium-endurance cutter. Her keel was laid in 1982 at Robert Derecktor Shipyard Inc. in Middletown, Rhode Island. She was launched in 1984 and formally commissioned in 1987. Her namesake is the first revenue cutter *Seneca*, which was operative from 1908 to 1936. Seneca is the sixth of thirteen 270-foot Famous-class cutters "designed to take the Coast Guard into the future."

The advanced technology used in her construction enables it to be an effective vessel for search and rescue (SAR) and maritime law enforcement (MLE) platforms. Her SCCS (Shipboard Command and Control System) allows operators to view or act on information from any of the ship's sensors, radar sources or radio transceivers. The *Seneca* serves as part of Operation New Frontier, the Coast Guard's operation to employ armed helicopters and nonlethal use of force technology to stop drug-laden go-fast vessels.

Christensen, a native of Sunapee, New Hampshire, supervises a crew of about one hundred on the *Seneca*. The Boston-berthed vessel is often assigned to southern Florida and the Caribbean to stop the importation of

Commander John Christensen stands in front of the *Seneca*, the 270-foot cutter that he commands out of Boston. The armed vessel is often routed to the Caribbean, where it patrols to halt drug smugglers. *Photo by Dyke Hendrickson.*

illegal drugs. The ship is prepared for trouble, and it carries heavy machine guns to get its message across.

Officials say *Seneca*'s actions contributed to the 100 percent interdiction rate during Operation New Frontier, making it the most successful counter-drug operation in Coast Guard history. Six drug-smuggling go-fast vessels were stopped; 4,475 pounds of cocaine and 11,710 pounds of marijuana with a street value of over $125 million were seized; and eighteen drug-trafficking suspects were arrested.

When at sea, *Seneca* uses a significant amount of technology to identify fast-moving boats that are smuggling cocaine. She also patrols Caribbean waters in search of vessels carrying would-be immigrants to southern Florida. Many boats are overloaded and unfit for travel. Christensen said his team views the interdiction of refugees as actually saving lives, as their makeshift vessels often sink before reaching southern Florida. The cutter can launch a Dolphin chopper from its deck or put speedy vessels over the side.

The crew aboard the *Seneca* returned in the fall of 2018 to their homeport of Boston following a fifty-day counter-drug patrol in the eastern Pacific. They patrolled international waters off the coast of Central America and South America in support of the Joint Interagency Task Force South.

Seneca intercepted four vessels suspected of smuggling illegal contraband; two of the vessels interdicted by *Seneca* were low-profile go-fast vessels, designed to traffic large quantities of illicit contraband by riding low in the water in an effort to evade detection.

Seneca also intercepted a fishing vessel suspected of international drug trafficking. After several hours of searching, the boarding team discovered a hidden compartment containing approximately five hundred kilograms of cocaine valued at $16.5 million.

"I am extremely proud of this crew and their efforts," said Christensen. "In just one interdiction, we seized over fifty times the amount of contraband seized along the southwest border in a given month. Yet we need more resources. The 220 metric tons of cocaine the Coast Guard seizes at sea per year represents only a small fraction of the total exports via maritime means."

Christensen got his nautical start when he attended the Massachusetts Maritime Academy. He learned how to drive ships and realized he had a love for the sea. After three years in the Navy—including service during the terrorist raids of September 2001—he joined the Coast Guard.

He has a wife and two children in coastal Connecticut and has served nineteen years in the Coast Guard. In the coming year, he will decide whether to retire after two decades or remain in the service. He says being the commanding officer of a cutter is a dream come true. "We have a good crew and knowledgeable leaders," Christensen said. "We like to be underway and doing important work."

The ship captain remarked that the Coast Guard offers much opportunity for individual advancement. He suggested he can do more for his country—and himself—in the Coast Guard than anywhere else.

Chapter 5

FROM MINNESOTA TO MIDDLE EAST TO NEW HAMPSHIRE

I t's said that benefits of the Coast Guard include travel and adventure. Amanda Fenstermacher, recently posted in Portsmouth, New Hampshire, can attest to the travel.

After joining the service in 2006, she has emerged as a versatile trainer of security teams as part of the International Mobile Training Branch. Her postings have included Brazil, where she helped train security teams prior to the Olympics and World Cup in 2016. She has also served in Djibouti, Haiti, Italy, Mexico, Peru and Uganda teaching courses including Port and Waterway Coast Security.

"It's a dream job, and I was fortunate to get it," said Fenstermacher, a native of Minnesota. "Some response teams in other countries don't have the resources that we do. I remember one group we worked with would siphon gas so they would have enough fuel for a training mission. You realize how lucky you are to be an American and in the Coast Guard."

Fenstermacher enlisted in the Coast Guard after trying community college. Following Coast Guard schooling, she served on a buoy tender out of Kodiak, Alaska. "After growing up in Minnesota, Kodiak wasn't that cold," said the affable Coastie. "It's on the water and maybe thirty degrees warmer than my hometown."

Her work in Alaska involved inspecting and cleaning buoys and other aids to navigation. Historians say that care of navigation aids is one of the most important—if underrated—missions that the Coast Guard performs. She said, "If not maintained, buoys will be lost. Without buoys, ships can run

Amanda Fenstermacher has been on assignments to almost a dozen countries in her role as a security instructor. She was recently based in Portsmouth, New Hampshire. *Photo by Dyke Hendrickson.*

aground." Indeed, even casual mariners need visual guidelines when plying New England waters.

In 2009, she got an assignment for more training in Yorktown, Virginia— in part because there was a berthing open for a woman. This led to training with the International Mobile Training Branch and much travel. After several years of teaching aspects of international port security, she was assigned overseas. Her ship was an escort in the Strait of Hormuz. Tensions were high. The Strait of Hormuz is between the Persian Gulf and the Gulf of Oman. It provides the only sea passage from the Persian Gulf to the open ocean and is one of the world's most strategically important waterways. At the narrowest, the strait has a width of twenty-nine nautical miles. Historians say about 35 percent of the world's petroleum passes through the strait, making it hugely important for America and other western countries.

Though no shots were fired on her craft while she was there, the memory of Nathan Bruckenthal was foremost on the minds of many. He was a Coast Guardsman who was killed in a suicide bombing while protecting nearby oil fields. Coast Guard historians have created a memorial of his time and service at the Coast Guard Museum in New London, Connecticut, among other places.

In 2015, Fenstermacher was posted to Portsmouth, New Hampshire, where she is qualified to pilot vessels including a forty-seven-foot search-and-rescue boat and a twenty-five-footer.

Though the Coast Guard has state-of-the-art technology, one of the station's recent rescues came as a result of a sighting from land. Observers at the Castle Hill station saw a kayak several hundred yards into the Piscataqua River. The craft seemed empty, but the Coast Guard decided to launch a vessel and check. Upon reaching the overturned craft, they found a kayaker under the vessel. He was without a paddle, life preserver or cold-weather clothing.

"He couldn't have lasted much longer," said Fenstermacher. "He had flipped and was in jeans and wearing just a thin coat even though it was winter. We got him to shore and then right to the hospital. He survived."

Fenstermacher said that Coast Guard personnel responding to life-threating situations of a craft on the water are trained to obtain a GPS location, ascertain the number of people on board, check for life jackets, learn the nature of distress, get a description of the vessel and find a cell phone number for possible triangulation. They also suggest that boaters and paddlers write their cell phone numbers on gear they wear or carry because it enhances their chances of being identified if they are lost.

If Fenstermacher has traveled much by sea in her career, she also uses the roads. Her husband, Travis Fenstermacher, is stationed near Providence, Rhode Island, where he serves as a maritime enforcement specialist with the Coast Guard. They've settled in the midway point of Littleton, Massachusetts, where they reconnoiter on weekends and during leaves. Both likely will be reassigned in coming years.

"I love my job in the Coast Guard," Fenstermacher said. "A crew can make or break a posting, and I have been fortunate to have been on a great ship, and I have had postings with fine people. My husband and I are planning the future, and there are a lot of options and opportunities. The Coast Guard has been a very good choice for me."

• MODERN COAST GUARD, PART II •

PRESENCE OF WOMEN HAS CHANGED FACE OF SERVICE

Chapter 6

Captain Claudia Gelzer and the History of Women in Coast Guard

W hen Claudia Gelzer was a student at the University of Maryland, she took several journalism courses. After getting out of the classroom and into the "real world," she got interested in maritime environmental issues. She wrote stories for class and the school newspaper. She did not enter the field of journalism. But she did become interested in the maritime environment, and much of her supervisory career in the Coast Guard has been involved in clean water and maritime regulation.

One of the Coast Guard's missions is enforcing environmental regulations, and Gelzer's work in New England often encompassed that. She retired in 2018 as captain of the Port of Boston. Part of her job description was "Officer in Charge of Marine Inspections."

"The environment is an important part of the job in New England," said Gelzer. "The Port of Boston has a great deal of traffic, from pleasure boats to very large tankers. If there is a spill or a boat sinking, we are there to be part of the cleanup."

In 2015, Gelzer assumed the duties as sector commander of Boston, where she oversaw every Coast Guard mission from the New Hampshire and Massachusetts border to Plymouth, Massachusetts. That region includes 227 miles of coastline and 200 nautical miles offshore.

She led a sector composed of nearly 350 active duty and civilian personnel, 120 Reservists and 1,000 Auxiliary members. The sector's sub-units include four small boat stations, a 110-foot and 87-foot patrol boat, a 65-foot icebreaking tug and one aids-to-navigation team.

"The extraordinary people of Massachusetts and members of Sector Boston proudly defined my tour," said Gelzer. "The port partners in Massachusetts and Boston are second to none; they like the Coast Guard and recognize its importance."

Gelzer, a native of Rye, New York, joined the Coast Guard in 1991. She graduated from Officer Candidate School and rose steadily. The start of her career coincided with the "early years" of women being part of the service.

"There were many times when I was the only women in the room of male officers," she said. "This was an environment of Type-A personalities, and I had to be assertive and persistent to make my views count." Her skills enabled her to be the top officer at the Port of Boston, meaning she supervised both commercial and recreational traffic in Boston Harbor.

"I never saved a life myself—that's not what officers generally do—but I was responsible for thousands of lives on the water every day," she said. "And when things went wrong and there was an accidental death [involved in Coast Guard waters], I was the one who made the call on survivors to convey our concern."

Reaching the rank of captain is a major achievement. At the age of fifty-three, when she retired, Gelzer said she would take some time off before perhaps entering the field of marine-environment safety.

Coast Guard captain Eric Doucette relieved her as commander of the Coast Guard Sector Boston in 2018 at a ceremony at Faneuil Hall in Boston.

Gelzer's notable career follows an institutional goal of recruiting more women for the Coast Guard. For decades, women had minor roles. For

Captain Claudia C. Gelzer, once the commander of Coast Guard Sector Boston, is attentive during a presentation in 2015. *U.S. Coast Guard photo by Petty Officer Third Class Ross Ruddell.*

instance, in the eighteenth and nineteenth centuries, numerous women served as lighthouse assistants and/or rescue-team members only. Their good deeds were usually tied to the roles of their fathers or husbands. Beginning during World War I, women began to have independent roles.

Coast Guard historians say Genevieve and Lucille Baker, nineteen-year-old twins, volunteered to serve with the Coast Guard during World War I. They were the first women to don Coast Guard uniforms, and they served at headquarters in Washington.

During World War II, the Coast Guard recruited women for the SPARs (Semper Paratus, Always Ready), a female corps similar to the Navy WAVES and the Army WACS. Almost twelve thousand women volunteered and served in the Coast Guard during the conflict.

After the war, women's military reserve branches were disbanded, typified by the proverbial Rosie the Riveter. During the Korean Conflict, from 1950 to 1953, the Coast Guard did not mobilize former SPARs. By 1956, the Coast Guard counted only twelve female officers and nine enlisted women out of thousands of service personnel, historians say. But with the development of the women's movement in the '70s, the opportunities expanded. In 1973, congressional legislation allowed women to serve alongside men on active duty in both the regular Coast Guard and Coast Guard Reserves. Under the 1973 legislation, the Coast Guard began to integrate women into its enlisted ranks.

In 1975, the service counted 420 enlisted women and 32 female officers among its active-duty personnel. In that year, the Coast Guard announced it would offer appointments to female applicants.

In 1976, the class of 1980 swabs at the Coast Guard Academy in New London included 38 women. It was the first time that a U.S. military service had accepted women to its academy. Three years later, the service counted 129 female officers, many of them Academy graduates, with 35 serving afloat and 5 serving as aviators.

In 1990, the service's "Women in the Coast Guard" study led to a systematic effort to support female recruiting and retention, including a new Women's Advisory Council. During operations Desert Shield and Desert Storm, three Port Security Units, with female personnel, were sent to the Persian Gulf. For the first time, female members received combat assignments, such as manning the .50-caliber heavy machine gun onboard Raider boats.

More female officers received afloat commands, including Katherine Tiongson, the first minority female skipper, who in 1991 took command of cutter *Bainbridge Island*. She retired as a captain and is the wife of Rear

Vice Admiral Sandra Stosz, now retired, served as superintendent of the Coast Guard Academy. *U.S. Coast Guard photo.*

Admiral Andrew Tiongson, who in 2018 commanded the First Coast Guard District.

The twenty-first century saw women reach the highest officer positions. OCS graduates led the way to top positions, including Vivien Crea, who in 2000 became the first woman to achieve flag rank. Later, in 2006, Crea was promoted to vice commandant of the Coast Guard, becoming the first woman to hold the second-highest position of any military service. And while serving as acting commandant, she was the first woman in U.S. history to oversee a military service.

Several Coast Guard Academy graduates have also achieved flag rank during this period, including Vice Admiral Sandra Stosz, who headed the Coast Guard Academy.

Today, over 5,800 women serve out of nearly 42,000 active-duty service members. While the percentage of active-duty women remains modest compared to total service figures, the proportion of women in the Coast Guard continues to grow.

Many Coast Guard "alums" go on to new civilian professions. "I am going to continue a career," said Gelzer. "I am still interested in the marine environment and may seek a position that involves regulation and natural resources."

Chapter 7

ONLY WOMAN AT MAINE OUTPOST

Meghan Cahoon, an enlistee in Rockland, Maine, graduated from Ohio Wesleyan University and plans to be a teacher. But for now, she enjoys mentoring other service members.

"I love to teach and mentor others," said Cahoon, whose formative years were spent in Montpelier, Vermont, and Rockport, Maine. "The people at the station are great, and we're really a family.

"Right now, I am the only woman of a team of about thirty-three. But I am comfortable. We work well together, and this has been a great place for me."

Cahoon is among the highest-ranking enlisted personnel at the station and often runs vessels and supervises crews.

The circumstance that she was the lone lady underlines an ongoing fact about Coast Guard life: almost every assignment is going to be top-heavy with men. Since their arrival as full-timers in the mid-'70s, women have been vastly in the minority. Several women interviewed for this book said they became interested when they checked the classified sections of their local newspaper and read ads that started with "Women Wanted."

The Coast Guard station in Rockland, Maine, has multiple missions. One is to run search-and-rescue operations and buoy-tending functions from its headquarters on the city pier, and another is to berth several cutters and tugs. Head of station in 2018 was Boatswain Second Class Hans Schultz.

The station has about thirty-three personnel, and much of their work is patrolling Penobscot Bay. It operates two forty-seven-foot rescue craft and

Meghan Cahoon was at one point the only woman on a thirty-three-member team at her Rockland, Maine station. She said she enjoys mentoring and teaching. *Dyke Hendrickson photo.*

a twenty-nine-foot harbor boat. It also hosts larger vessels that can go far into the ocean.

One craft tied up in Rockland is the 175-foot *Abbie Burgess*, a high-tech buoy tender. Other working vessels include the *Thunder Bay*, a 140-foot tug. It does ice-breaking and lighthouse repair. The *Tackle*, a 65-foot harbor tug, carries out ice-breaking chores in the Penobscot and Kennebec Rivers.

Rockland hosts an extensive lighthouse museum that references many Coast Guard sites.

Chapter 8

A View from Quiet, Coastal Jonesport, Maine

T he following is an interview with Boatswain's Mate Third Class Steph Horvat at Coast Guard Station Jonesport, Maine. This profile was created by Yeoman Second Class Courtney Myers as part of the Coast Guard's online series about enlisted empowerment.

What is your favorite part of your job?

I love being underway. Any day I can get out on the water is a good day. There is a spot in my area of responsibility where there are rock faces on either side of the boat. The channel is about 50 yards wide but about 110 feet deep. This is my favorite area. There are pine trees on top of the rock faces and a lighthouse on the very end of the right rock outcropping. I have that lighthouse on my arm as part of my nautical tattoo sleeve. I am also the social media coordinator for my unit, so I enjoy telling stories about the station to the public. I went to college for TV broadcasting, so it takes me back to my college days.

What has been the most memorable moment of your career?

I've been in a little less than three years, but I'd have to say taking my coxswain board in August. I had such a hard time trying to qualify, and taking my board represented a mountain peak. I'm teetering on the edge of it still. I'm currently waiting on some weather for a check ride, but the new command has been great about having me take my time and really get comfortable with driving.

Steph Horvat was assigned to one of the quietest stations in New England: Jonesport, Maine. She said the Coast Guard has provided a valuable learning experience. *U.S. Coast Guard photo.*

Did you ever feel like giving up? What made you keep pushing?

When I was trying to qualify as a coxswain for the forty-seven-foot motor lifeboat, I kept facing roadblock after roadblock on sign-offs, and I almost went back to school to become a machinery technician. I still joke about it, but now that I am on the last step to becoming a coxswain, I want it. Honestly, my mom and friends are what kept me going. My mom was (and still is) so proud of me; I couldn't let her down. My friends kept me pushing because they said I am a fighter and no matter what, I would never give up on my dreams. Well, my dream was to join the Coast Guard and serve my country. In the process, I'm trying to get as many qualifications as I can. Coxswain just happens to be the biggest one I've had to face so far.

Do you have a hobby that you enjoy outside of work?

I love to write. I'm currently working on a book about a female in present day that lost her lover but vows to find him in another life. Then it goes into the 1800s to a female who ran away from her privileged lifestyle to become a pirate. She, of course, meets a pirate and falls in love with him. But the admiral she ran away from is chasing her across the seven seas. Think of *Pirates of the Caribbean* meets *Time Traveler's Wife*. I also love to visit and research lighthouses of the area. Another big passion of mine is sailing. However, I have not sailed since early college. If I could get my hands on a small sailboat, I would be doing that as much as I can. I also enjoy horseback riding, which I have not done for a few years as well. Boats and horses are just too expensive for someone who moves every two to four years. Plus, my husband is a little afraid of both. Oh well. Maybe when I retire in eighteen years.

Is there anything particular you do outside of your Coast Guard service to maintain your personal identity?

I'm stationed in Jonesport, Maine, so there's not much to do. I do go hiking, camping and kayaking a lot in the summertime. I'm also still involved in a Sea Cadet unit as an officer. One weekend a month, I drill with the cadets and teach them about the maritime services and offer as much leadership as I can to the high school cadets.

What advice would you give to young women thinking about joining the service?

Do it! The Coast Guard is a great opportunity for females....The Coast Guard allows me to do anything, from sanding and painting the boat to helping fix an engine.

Chapter 9

A COMMANDER IN CONNECTICUT

VALERIE BOYD'S POSTINGS HAVE INCLUDED NEW LONDON, NEW HAVEN

T he devastation of Hurricane Katrina in 2005 put pressure on numerous municipal, state and federal agencies and the U.S. Coast Guard. One of the young offers at the forefront of the service's initiative was then-lieutenant Valerie Ann Boyd.

Boyd, now a commander based in New Haven, was just a few years out of the Coast Guard Academy with a degree in civil engineering. She graduated in 2001. She served as Sector New Orleans liaison officer and lead Coast Guard representative on the Joint Search and Rescue Task Force at the Louisiana State Office of Homeland Security and Emergency Preparedness. Coast Guard officials commended her for her work. In an official statement, ranking officers said, "Her expert coordination with fellow search and rescue agencies resulted in more than 24,000 rescues and 9,000 medical evacuations."

Hurricane Katrina was not a New England event, of course, but hundreds from this region and others were deployed to help those in the New Orleans area. Katrina was a damaging hurricane, but the subsequent flooding from Lake Pontchartrain into the city resulted in one of the greatest domestic disasters in U.S. history. The Coast Guard was lauded; the Federal Emergency Management Agency was derided for what critics called inefficiency and slowness to act.

"Katrina presented huge problems, and I was very junior then," said Boyd, a native of Whitesboro, New York, near Utica. "At that time, I followed my training and did what I had learned.

Commander Valerie Boyd is one of the top officers at the station in New Haven, Connecticut. *Dyke Hendrickson photo.*

"We had many calls from people in critical situations, and we responded with other agencies as rapidly as we could. At one point, I was stationed near the Superdome (which took in many homeless and desperate residents). I thought those with the National Guard and FEMA were very effective. And the Coast Guard did very valuable work."

Historians say that one problem that FEMA faced with Hurricane Katrina was that it could not deploy resources until state and federal authorities issued orders. Perhaps because of political misunderstandings, some federal agencies appeared slow to respond. In the post-Katrina era, federal agencies now have the authority to "pre-deploy," or head toward trouble without waiting for approval by political entities.

Boyd said she got interested in the Coast Guard late in high school, when her mother told her she did not have the money to send her to college. Boyd, a good student and superior athlete, came from a family populated by Navy veterans. But she applied to the Coast Guard Academy. While moving smoothly through her academics, she also excelled in soccer. During her senior year, she was captain of the Bears varsity.

Upon graduation, she reported to a Coast Guard unit in Portsmouth, Virginia, as an engineer officer in training. She served as damage control assistant and assistant engineer officer. In addition to engineering duties, Boyd qualified as a quartermaster of the watch and deck watch officer.

In 2003, she reported to New Orleans, where she served as assistant chief of marine environmental responses and earned the Coast Guard Marine Safety Professional Pin. Boyd advanced to serve as command duty officer and subsequently the command center supervisor in the newly established

New Orleans Command Center, where she was responsible for the daily operations in one of the nation's busiest port complexes. She was ready when Hurricane Katrina hit in late August 2005. "The situation was serious, and the calls for help didn't seem to stop," she said. "I am proud of how our team worked with others."

She departed Sector New Orleans in 2007 to attend the University of New Haven, where she earned a master of arts degree in industrial and organizational psychology. In August 2008, she reported to the Coast Guard Academy in New London, where she served as Foxtrot Company officer in the Commandant of Cadets Division, "managing the good order and discipline for more than one thousand prospective Coast Guard officers."

In July 2011, she went to the Marine Safety Unit Texas City, where she served as the response department head. From July 2014 to July 2016, she served as commanding officer of the Miami Military Entrance Processing Station.

Later, Boyd reported to Washington, D.C., to serve as the Coast Guard liaison officer to FEMA. Also, she served as the Coast Guard's representative to the National Response Coordination Center during Hurricane Matthew in 2016 and Hurricanes Harvey, Irma and Maria in 2017.

"I've often been in the right place at the right time," the officer said in the summer of 2018. "I've had excellent training, and I make every effort to work with others."

Though it's hard to believe she's had the time, Boyd is the mother of three young girls. "My husband (also in the Coast Guard) and I have been stationed near each other," she said. "The Coast Guard has made an effort to accommodate couples in the service."

Boyd's personal awards include the Defense Meritorious Service Medal, two Meritorious Service Medals, four Commendation Medals, two Achievement Medals, a Coast Guard Letter of Commendation, the Armed Forces Service Medal, the Humanitarian Service Medal and seventeen Meritorious Team Commendations.

Chapter 10

A CHIEF BOATSWAIN'S MATE
REMEMBERS A RESCUE OFF
MARTHA'S VINEYARD

Kathleen Wedge retired from the Coast Guard in 2011 after twenty years of service. During those years, she traveled the world and rose high in the enlisted ranks, retiring as a chief boatswain's mate (E-7). After retirement, she received a bachelor's degree in business administration from Hawaii Pacific University in Honolulu, one of the cities in which she served. She is a native of Billerica, Massachusetts, and has resettled in that area.

She appears to be an example of a retired veteran who enjoyed her career and has moved on to new challenges. Wedge now is involved in craft and commerce in eastern Massachusetts.

Wedge recently reflected on her career by saying, "I loved working in search and rescue and law enforcement, and I relished the opportunity to educate the public on the importance of boating safety and proper navigational skills. I thoroughly enjoyed mentoring junior personnel to further their Coast Guard careers."

Wedge spent more than a decade on the sea and became accustomed to rescues of all kinds. Some of her final assignments included the USCGC *Waesche*, out of Alameda, California; the Motor Lifeboat Station in Bodega Bay, California; the Coast Guard small-boats station in Monterey, California; Sector Honolulu in Hawaii; on the USCGC *Washington*; and on the USCGC *Monomoy* in New England.

Thoughts of staying in for more than twenty years were put aside after she developed a medical condition known as fibromyalgia, an ailment marked by frequent pain.

Her career was marked by advancement and achievement, but constant reassignment might have hampered her ability to develop permanent relationships. "I was engaged three times but never married," the thoughtful retiree said. "In each case, we faced long separations and new living arrangements, especially if you go out to sea, as I did."

The New England veteran, who sometimes attends events of the Coast Guard Auxiliary, said that she would recommend a career in the Coast Guard to young women. "There is travel, adventure and the opportunity to get support for educational goals," she said. "I tested well early in my career, and I had much training, which resulted in advancement. I had hoped to become the highest-ranking women's noncommissioned officer.

"I didn't achieve that, but I enjoyed my career and felt I was making a contribution to this country."

Wedge's time at sea meant that she was involved in "real life" rescues. She provided this synopsis of a rescue in New England. Much of it was written by John Leaning, a reporter for the *Cape Cod Times*, in November 1999. Wedge was working onboard during this rescue.

Wedge was a quartermaster in the late '90s on the *Monomoy*, a 110-foot Island Class cutter based at Woods Hole, Massachusetts. It was mid-November 1999, and the first distress call came at about 1:30 p.m.

The story said, "A 42-foot fishing vessel [the *Chrissie*], south of Nomans Land, a deserted island south of Martha's Vineyard, was calling for help. The boat was taking on water, and even in the raspy, broken radio broadcast, you could hear the fear in the caller's voice. 'We can't keep up with the water,' the voice said over the radio.

"Coast Guard: 'Do you have survival gear? Take the EPIRB (emergency position indicator radio beacon) with you if you have to abandon ship,' radio operator Altino D. Carvalho of New Bedford, Massachusetts, told the fishing boat captain."

On the bridge of the *Monomoy*, skipper Lieutenant Mark J. Fedor ordered an increase in speed to fifteen knots, sending the sharp white bow of the cutter slicing through four- to six-foot seas. As the cutter sped to the rescue, Coast Guard crew members on the bridge used grab bars to keep their balance. White water from swells would envelop the forward deck, forcing anyone on the outside bridge to duck to avoid getting drenched by the stinging spray.

The story said, "Fedor listened to the radio exchange, contacted his commander and then ordered more speed, to 23 knots. The powerful twin diesels growled in response to the throttle signal, and the ship surged forward.

Kat Wedge rose high in the enlisted ranks while engaging in several harrowing rescues. *Photo from collection of Kathleen Wedge.*

"While Quartermaster First Class Kathy Wedge pulled out a standard search-and-rescue report form to keep detailed records of actions and responses during the mission, others on the bridge plotted the course, kept binoculars to their eyes and monitored the radio calls between rescuers and the sinking ship."

The pilot of a Coast Guard Falcon aircraft dispatched from Air Station Cape Cod radioed the fishing boat captain. "We will be dropping a pump in 30 seconds." At 2:05 p.m., the pump had been delivered to the Coast Guard craft as the fishing boat was still taking on water.

"Sinking from the stern, the skipper was trying to prevent the following seas from surging over the transom and flooding the boat. He was heading into the seas, pitching the bow into the coming swells. The motion made it difficult for the three-man crew struggling to work the pumps."

Fedor sent out a crew to the forward deck to prepare to launch the *Monomoy's* seventeen-foot rigid-hulled inflatable. Bouncing over the rough seas, the rescue boat, with another portable pump, made it to the *Chrissie*. Three crew members from the rescue craft transferred the pump onto the fishing boat.

The Coast Guard personnel who boarded the *Chrissie* managed to stabilize the flooding. They concentrated on the main center hold to keep the boat afloat. They worked to patch leaks in the hull, and they kept Fedor informed. Group Woods Hole, Fedor and group commander Captain Russell Webster discussed the situation by radio. Webster emphasized the importance of determining the danger point when everyone must leave the *Chrissie*. "We're talking about people here, not equipment," the captain told Fedor.

With help from the Coast Guard Marine Safety Office in Providence, Fedor and Webster worked out a plan to protect the crew and save the boat if possible. Decision No. 1: head the *Chrissie* to Martha's Vineyard, thirty-two miles away. Though Block Island was only eighteen miles away, it was determined that heading into the pounding sea was more dangerous than having the sea to the stern. Decision No. 2: keep everyone on the *Chrissie* on deck in case they had to get off the boat in a hurry. And everyone must have on their survival gear.

The rigid-hulled inflatable was returned to the *Monomoy*. The *Chrissie* began moving slowly to its destination. A forty-seven-foot Coast Guard vessel had arrived from Woods Hole, and it stayed alongside the fishing boat. The *Chrissie* made only six and a half knots. And then, about fifteen miles south of the Vineyard, it had engine trouble and had to be towed. It was dark now, and the following sea put the boats into an unpleasant rolling motion.

The story said, "The last excitement came about 1:30 a.m., when the 47-footer transferred the boarding party on the *Chrissie* back to the *Monomoy*. Cruising at about 9 knots, the two vessels came within a foot of each other. They stepped over the surging sea onto the mother vessel.

"The *Chrissie* was docked, ready for repairs. The 47-footer turned and began its journey back to Woods Hole. When all personnel were secured, the *Monomoy* turned and headed into the night to resume its patrol."

• MODERN COAST GUARD, PART III •

SERVICE ON SEA AND ON LAND

Chapter 11

HEARTLAND NATIVE REMEMBERS ASSISTING PLANE, VESSEL

Not every Coastie is raised near the New England coast, and that includes Paul Dilger. He is a native of Bismarck, North Dakota, but he traveled the world before retiring to Rockland, Maine, as a chief warrant officer.

"I was raised on a farm, and after some junior college, I was working in a Holiday Inn in Minnesota," said Dilger, who left the service after thirty years in 2007. "I thought I was doing very well, supervising their lounge and working very hard. I asked for a raise. The manager came back to me and said he would offer an increase of ten cents per hour. That was so low that I started looking for another position."

Dilger researched the different services and thought the Coast Guard would work. He had spent many hours sailing on lakes in Minnesota and liked the idea of perhaps driving a ship.

"When I was in boot camp in Alameda [California], I was like a lot of guys, wondering what I had got myself into. But I got through it and began liking it," he said.

Dilger went to quartermaster school in Florida and had a career that included service on numerous vessels, including the 210-foot *Courageous*, the 95-foot *Cape Horn*, the 82-foot Expo, the 180-foot *Sassafras* and the 175-foot *Baltimore*.

He also served in a general operations category in a joint rescue operations team in Honolulu. "In Hawaii, we had a situation where a pilot was heading to Christmas Island," said the soft-spoken Dilger. "He couldn't find his way with his navigation tools. We were able to determine his course and speed and provide direction on the radio. He finally made it, and back in Hawaii, we all felt good about helping him."

On another occasion, his vessel saved a pleasure boat about one hundred miles off Charleston, South Carolina. "There were four in the water, with no life belts," the retired seaman said. "It was fortunate we were close enough to help before the exposure got to them."

Dilger is currently chairman of the board of the Maine Lighthouse Museum in Rockland, a well-appointed venue that includes a large section on the Coast Guard. He came to Rockland for the first time in about 1992, aboard the 133-foot *White Lupine*. He later served on the *Abby Burgess* there and decided to settle in that coastal town. He married and opted to stay after putting in thirty years.

Rockland is a community of about 7,200. It calls itself the lobster capital of the country. It is home to the Maine Lobster Festival, a celebration held annually in honor of the town's primary export: lobster.

Rockland also is home to the Farnsworth Art Museum, a world-famous art gallery containing paintings by Andrew Wyeth and other well-known New

Paul Dilger, who spent a full career in the Coast Guard, now heads the board of the Maine Lighthouse Museum in Rockland, Maine. *Dyke Hendrickson photo.*

England artists. Rockland's main street features numerous small shops and businesses, including coffee shops, bookstores, art supply stores, restaurants, organic markets, computer repair stores and toy stores. Penobscot Bay, which Rockland borders, is known as one of the best recreational sailing grounds in the world. The city's breakwater, almost a mile long, also draws tourists.

Rockland is a departure point for the Maine State Ferry Service to the islands of Penobscot Bay.

"Rockland has had a renaissance in recent years, and it's an amazing place to live," said Dilger, whose "second career" is that of a transportation manager for a local Lowe's outlet. "We have restaurants, boating, art galleries and some great activities.

"The museum keeps me busy; we have people coming from all over the world."

The retired Coastie said that during his service, a major satisfaction was mentoring young people. "Saving people was important. But also, I enjoyed teaching our newcomers and watching them grow," he said. "As they worked and trained, they got more confidence and became sharp, on-the-ball people.

"I look back, and I remember it started for me because I was only offered a ten-cent-an-hour raise. So I joined the Coast Guard and saw many parts of the country. I'm pleased with my decision."

Chapter 12

A Rescue Broken Off
but Then a Fatal Moment
Near Gloucester

Ralph Stevens served just four years in the Coast Guard (1975–79), but he was part of one of the most memorable—if unfortunate—events in Coast Guard history in New England. A pilot boat with five aboard sank in the Blizzard of 1978. All were lost.

Stevens, assigned to the station in Gloucester, Massachusetts, in the late '70s, was part of a mission in which the Coast Guard made the right decision. A rescue was cancelled.

"It was a terrible storm," said Stevens, retired from employment with the state and a part-time bartender at the Park Lunch restaurant in Newburyport, Massachusetts. "People even today remember the snowy roads and cars that got stuck, but on the ocean, it was twenty-five- to thirty-foot waves and winds at maybe fifty knots.

"We got a mayday call from a tanker in trouble off Gloucester, and we started out in a forty-one-footer. But we couldn't see because of the snow and wind, and it was decided by an officer that we would not be able to find the boat under these conditions. We didn't leave the harbor."

A local pilot boat heard the chatter on its radio. It did respond. It was the *Can Do*, a powerful fifty-footer.

The tanker, the *Global Home,* was outside Gloucester Harbor, and its captain felt the vessel was in distress. The storm was fierce and the seas were high. But it was a very large ship, and historians in retrospect wonder how a small vessel could have helped.

But the crew of the *Can Do* heard the same alarms as the Coast Guard, and it left Gloucester toward Salem Sound, a few miles to the south. Historians say the crew was headed by captain Frank Quirk. Because all were capable seamen, those who heard that the *Can Do* was missing felt the sturdy vessel would return.

But this was the worst storm in a century.

The Coast Guard did not go out. The *Can Do* did. No one returned.

"When something like that happens, some people operate on adrenalin rather than taking a step back to analyze the situation," Stevens said years later. "I understand how in some circumstances there is no time to waste, but in the case of this six-hundred-foot tanker, it wasn't going anywhere. We took a step back, and before putting our boat out on the rescue, the officers paused and looked at the big picture and let common sense dictate action.

"Going out during a blizzard is dangerous. I was on the same forty-one-foot Coastie boat when we rushed to save the *Chester Poling* in another tough situation, and I'm lucky we made it back from that one.

Ralph Stevens served a four-year hitch out of Gloucester, Massachusetts, and survived the Blizzard of '78 there. Here he stands at the memorial for lost fishermen in Newburyport, Massachusetts. *Dyke Hendrickson photo.*

"Losing guys on the *Can Do* was awful. It was heartbreaking then, and it is still heartbreaking now."

The Coast Guard's responsibilities in Gloucester include supervision of the harbor, the adjacent ocean and also narrow rivers.

Many books and movies have revolved around the station, most notably the story of the fishing vessel *Andrea Gail* that was the basis of *The Perfect Storm*, the best-selling book by Sebastian Junger.

Stevens, a native of Manchester, New Hampshire, joined the Coast Guard when the option to attend college did not work out. He did well in basic training at Cape May, New Jersey, and spent much of his time in Gloucester.

He did not make it a career. "I probably should have stayed in," said Stevens. "I liked the service, I liked the guys, and Gloucester was a good place."

Stevens spent his career near the water, though. He was a state employee of the clam-cleansing operation on Plum Island, the barrier island off Newburyport. Clam lovers on the North Shore of Massachusetts likely benefited from the fact that technicians like Stevens were cleaning clams, which in recent years have been compromised by pollution spawned by the Merrimack River. Numerous mill cities, including several in New Hampshire and Lowell, Lawrence, Haverhill, Amesbury and Newburyport itself, have cited wastewater treatment plants on the river as the cause. Restrictions have made water cleaner in recent years. But when heavy rainstorms overwhelm the plants' capacity, effluent flows downriver and clam flats are affected by the fouled water.

Newburyport has improved much during Stevens's tenure there. City officials in the '70s and '80s decided to use urban renewal money to rehabilitate the downtown. Newburyport opted to save old brick buildings, many erected after the Great Fire of 1811. The city of Newburyport has been recognized by national historical groups as a leader in its vision to preserve the Federal architecture of the past.

Although bold action and courageous acts are lauded by Coast Guard leaders, officers now have complex risk-assessment propositions to determine if their vessels should respond to emergencies in heavy weather. "The Blizzard of '78 was one emergency the Coast Guard took action a little later," said Stevens. "It saved our lives. I just feel bad about the crew of the *Can Do*."

Chapter 13

Coast Guard's "Inland" Stations Include Burlington, Vermont

M any Americans do not know that the Coast Guard maintains stations on lakes, rivers and other non-ocean locations. In New England, a station in Burlington, Vermont, anchors Lake Champlain. Inland states including Ohio, Michigan, Indiana, Tennessee, Illinois, Wisconsin and Minnesota have vibrant outposts. Indeed, a significant part of America's trade takes place because of transportation opportunities on the Great Lakes, Mississippi River and other non–New England waterways.

Some say one of the most desirable postings is Burlington. It's cold in winter but delightful in summer. Some who are posted there say they have "amnesia" when it comes to remembering winter.

It might be argued, too, that there are fewer frenetic moments in a given year because the winter ice on Lake Champlain keeps boat traffic to a minimum. There are ice rescues, to be sure. And teams drill constantly to practice the most successful methods of rescuing those who have gone through the ice. But there are slow winter days in Burlington because boaters have gone into a kind of hibernation.

Because the lake is adjacent to Canada, responsibilities include monitoring boat traffic for illegal immigrants and importation of drugs. Personnel there inspect pleasure craft, enforce environmental regulations and embark on search-and-rescue missions. They provide maintenance to navigation aids, such as buoys.

Two Coasties gather in front of their station in Burlington, Vermont. They are Chris Batton, *left*, and Jason Balmer. *Dyke Hendrickson photo.*

In winter, they are often tasked to rescue and retrieve vehicles that have crashed through the ice when drivers are foolish enough to try to traverse the (almost) frozen lake.

Coast Guard Station Burlington was established in 1948 as a four-man station. A modern facility was built on the waterfront in 1993 and now has about three dozen personnel stationed there. They operate vessels including a twenty-five-foot Defender Class boat, a forty-nine-foot buoy-utility vessel and a trailerable aids-to-navigation craft.

I traveled there in the spring of 2018 and interviewed two enlisted members, Chris Batton and Jason Balmer. Both men have been in the Coast Guard for about eighteen years.

Batton's first day in the service was September 11, 2001, and he said that the terrorist attacks put all Coast Guard stations on what might be called agitated alert. "My training was accelerated so our class of recruits could be put on guard duty almost immediately," said Batton. "It was a period of tension because on the first day, at least, no one knew exactly what we were dealing with."

The two said that many people they meet don't know exactly what the Coast Guard does. Also, they indicated the Coast Guard does not receive the credit it often deserves from the public and/or media. This is an opinion held by many members.

Numerous enlisted personnel approaching their twentieth year of service are thinking about what they will do in the future. Both Batton and Balmer said they are considering transitioning to other first responder positions, such as firefighter or emergency support. But they said they might stay in the service.

Chapter 14

A Career on Land Reaching to
South Portland, Maine

W hen Lori Fields was weighing her options after high school in central Washington in the early '90s, she noticed a classified ad in the local newspaper: "Women Wanted." In many communities, this might have been a call for cocktail waitresses or exotic dancers, but it turned out that the Coast Guard was recruiting. Fields responded, and a career as a Coastie was born.

"There weren't many jobs in my community, and I was not in college," said Fields, who recently spent several years in South Portland, Maine. "I followed up on the ad, went to Spokane to talk with the Coast Guard people and after three hours I was in.

"I went off to boot camp and kept remembering to read *The Helmsman* whenever I got nervous. I was in pretty good shape for the marching and physical fitness work, and I got used to the routine."

Fields recalled that there were about 150 people in her division. About 10 were women. Several of her supervisors were women. If anything, they were tougher on the females. "The guys were easier to work with. With some of the women in command, there seemed to be a pushback against females. They seemed to say, 'I'm not your sister, I'm not your friend.'"

Like others before her, she spent about eight weeks in barracks. At the conclusion of boot camp, she got to choose her career direction and chose vocations on land. By 2018, she had reached the rank of command master chief, a lofty post for an enlisted Coastie. For her, this involves work such as pay, personnel and human resources tasks.

Lori Fields has been a valuable asset in South Portland, Maine. Much of her career has been on land rather aboard vessels. *U.S. Coast Guard photo.*

Fields until recently was assigned to Sector Northern New England in South Portland, a community across Casco Bay from better-known Portland, Maine. The station is on Casco Bay, which hosts much commercial traffic as well as recreational vessels that cruise the coast of Maine. In recent years, huge cruise ships have visited the port in summer. It is part of Sector Northern New England, which has nineteen subunits and over 1,100 Active, Civilian, Reserve and Auxiliary personnel. Coasties carry out missions across Maine, New Hampshire, Vermont and northeastern New York.

Coast Guard officials say the area spans five thousand miles of coastline and eleven thousand square nautical miles of water. It includes numerous coast and river ports, including energy depots in Portland and Portsmouth, New Hampshire. With over one thousand deep-draft vessels arriving annually, the ports account for the movement of significant bulk and container freight. In addition, many ferries and tour boats operate in the region, transporting millions of passengers and serving as vital links to island communities and bordering states.

Boat building remains a strong regional tradition, with new vessels constructed each year. Other features of the sector's area of responsibility include joint protection and response missions along the Canadian border and the continued support and rapport shared with local Native American tribal communities.

Recruited in 1992, Fields got married in 1994 to another Coastie. She indicated that an administrative career would be easier for them to develop a family.

Her postings have included Port Angeles, Washington; Hawaii (1995–98); Astoria, Oregon (1998–2002); Seattle (2002–6); Command Station Pacific (2006–7); Anchorage (2007–9); Seattle (2009–13); Petaluma, California (2013–15); and South Portland, Maine (2015–18).

Fields has moved forward in the ranks, but not without observing some awkward moments. "We were on a polar ice breaker off Alaska, and a Russian fishing boat broke down," she said. "Our vessel went over to help. Our top officer was a woman. But the captain of the Russian boat wouldn't talk to her. He'd only talk to a guy. So our executive officer got the job. I guess they don't have many women in the higher ranks on Russian vessels because he didn't seem to understand that our top-ranking officer was a woman."

About her career, Fields said, "I am pleased with the Coast Guard. I would recommend it to other women. It's an organization that values females, and there are a lot of opportunities here."

Chapter 15

GETTING AN EDUCATION, RUNNING A STATION IN NEW HAMPSHIRE

Years ago, there was a saying in the Coast Guard that "you have to go out, but you don't have to come back." This is a dated directive because risk assessment has become a key element of rescue missions, says Chief Warrant Officer John Harker.

Harker has served as commanding officer of Station Portsmouth, New Hampshire, at Castle Hill. The Connecticut native is also a student of risk assessment and how it relates to rescue missions.

"Crews in the past would go out in high seas and heavy winds because there was a tradition," said Harker. "Now, leaders make assessment on the safety of the mission and the chances for success. We value our rescue teams. We still go out in bad conditions, but we consider what can go wrong and why. We look at other options before launching."

In the Coast Guard's words, "This unofficial motto dates to an 1899 U.S. Lifesaving Service regulation, which states in part, 'In attempting a rescue... he will not desist from his efforts until by actual trial, the impossibility of effecting a rescue is demonstrated. The statement of the keeper that he did not use the boat because the sea or surf was too heavy will not be accepted, unless attempts to launch it were actually made and failed.'" (Note: The Life-Saving Service merged with the Revenue Cutter Service in 1915 to form what we know as the U.S. Coast Guard.)

Harker is a leader who has taken advantage of educational possibilities and ways to improve himself. He might even be an example of the good that can happen when taking advantage of Coast Guard benefits.

Commander John Harker has spent much time in New England, including here in Portsmouth, New Hampshire. *Dyke Hendrickson photo.*

Harker left the College of Charleston in South Carolina before graduating. But once in the Coast Guard, he earned an associate's degree from Nichols College in Dudley, Massachusetts, and a bachelor's diploma from Endicott College in Beverly, Massachusetts. In the winter of 2017–18, the thoughtful leader was pursuing a graduate degree from Northeastern University (online) in homeland security/emergency management.

"The Coast Guard offers great opportunities to those who want to take advantage," the chief warrant officer said. "I am getting an education with nothing out of pocket regarding payment."

Indeed, in an era when student loans can threaten the early post-graduate years of college graduates, many young people are joining the Coast Guard with the expectation of earning degrees at minimal expense.

Harker was posted to New Hampshire in 2018. Because it is perched on land where the Piscataqua River meets the Atlantic, the Portsmouth station is tasked with numerous responsibilities. It is involved in search-and-rescue missions, of course, and monitoring fishing craft and pleasure boats. In recent years, a Coast Guard vessel might investigate a troubled vessel and not take the assignment itself. A leader might recommend that the captain contact a private company like TowBoatUSA rather than offer service itself. This is because crews want to be available should a more serious situation arise.

Though the size of the New England fishing fleet has diminished in recent years, there are still many lobster vessels and fishing craft that ply the waters. Coast Guard officials work closely with the National Oceanic and

Atmospheric Administration. They often board fishing boats to make sure they have been inspected and are in good working order.

Large tankers carrying gas and oil for New England homes and businesses dock in Portsmouth. Coast Guard personnel must board them and search their holds for contraband and weapons.

And the Portsmouth Naval Shipyard, a major servicer of military vessels, is at the mouth. Security is a key issue. Portsmouth Naval Shipyard's primary mission is the overhaul, repair and modernization of Los Angeles class submarines. This includes a full spectrum of in-house support, from engineering services and production shops to off-site support. Executives say their services fulfill a multifaceted assortment of fleet requirements.

"Since the September 11 attacks, the Coast Guard has taken on more security roles," said Harker. "We are responsible for the protection of numerous interests here in New Hampshire."

The station also covers southern Maine and the North Shore of Massachusetts. It maintains two forty-seven-foot surf boats and a personnel complement of about forty.

Women are among those at the Portsmouth station. In Harker's two decades in the service, a major change has been the increased presence of women. "The women are great assets to the service," said Harker, who enlisted in 2000. "They have been excellent team members in Portsmouth."

Harker has not finalized his plans for a career. He will be in for twenty, and most careers must end after thirty years. For the moment, he is both supervising the station and working on an advanced degree in a field that will always be required: national security.

"When I came into the Coast Guard, I had barely been in a boat," he said. "But once in the service, I found I had an affinity for the water." He also enjoys leading a team and hearing the opinions of others before making a decision.

Harker said he joined the Coast Guard to be of service to his country. This has ranged from saving small vessels in distress to escorting arriving tankers into port. Also, his team stresses safety on the water.

Perhaps because he has family in Gloucester and Beverly, Massachusetts, his deployments have included Boston, Cape Cod and Provincetown. He served one overseas year in Bahrain.

"I joined to help people and make a positive impact on lives," said Harker. "I value the education I am receiving and feel that I will be prepared for other roles when I leave the Coast Guard."

Chapter 16

COMMANDING OFFICER OF BUOY TENDER OPERATES OUT OF RHODE ISLAND

O ne of the most important—if underappreciated—vessels in the Coast Guard fleet is the buoy tender. Lieutenant Commander Greg Batchelder is the commanding officer of the *Juniper*, a buoy tender berthed in Newport, Rhode Island. His vessel is 225 feet long and carries a crew of about forty-five.

The vessel replaces or repairs buoys and signals in U.S. waters. It is also equipped to help clean up after oil spills in New England waters, and it can serve as a search-and-rescue asset and as a law enforcement vessel if called into action.

"This is an important job, and it supports both commercial traffic and recreational boating," said Batchelder, a Connecticut native. "Aids to navigation keep commerce flowing.

"We also help keep oil coming to New England states because we are an icebreaker in winter, making waterways navigable for tankers bringing in heating fuel.

"Regarding buoys and navigation, it seems like no one cares what we do unless something goes wrong. But this is an important function of the Coast Guard."

When the new republic started upgrading coastal assets to improve trade in 1789–90, President George Washington and Congress appropriated money for buoys and lighthouses to reduce the number of shipping calamities. Or in the words of Coast Guard historians, "On Aug. 7, 1789, an act of Congress, the first to make any provisions for public works, created the Lighthouse Establishment, when it accepted title to, and joined jurisdiction over, the 12 lighthouses then in existence, and provided that 'the necessary support, maintenance and repairs of all lighthouses, beacons, buoys and public piers erected, placed, or sunk before the passing of this act, at the entrance of, or within any bay, inlet, harbor, or port of the United States, for rendering the navigation thereof easy and safe, shall be defrayed out of the treasury of the United States.'"

Prior to this time, the buoys and lighthouses had been paid for, built and administered first by the colonies and then the states. In the modern era, the Coast Guard maintains about 4,800 buoys in the First Coast Guard District (New England, New York and northern New Jersey). That represents more than one-third of the national total of 12,600 buoys. The First District maintains six buoy tenders, the most of any of the service's districts.

If a buoy is malfunctioning, the *Juniper* travels to the site and identifies the problem. The task of the buoy tender appears to require patience—and lifting power. When a buoy has to be removed, a heavy crane on deck pulls the whole apparatus on deck—and that includes the buoy's anchor and connecting chains. Buoys that come out of New England waters are refurbished by private contractors in South Weymouth, Massachusetts.

Lieutenant Commander Greg Batchelder commands the *Juniper*, berthed in Newport, Rhode Island. He is a veteran in the use of buoy tenders. *Dyke Hendrickson photo.*

Batchelder graduated from the Coast Guard Academy in 2006, earning a degree in management, with honors, after short stints at Penn State and St. Lawrence University.

His first assignment was communications officer and later first lieutenant on USCGC *Dauntless* (WMEC 624) in Galveston, Texas, where he conducted alien migrant interdiction, counter narcotics and living marine resource patrols.

In 2008, Batchelder transferred to Mobile to serve as operations officer on USCGC *Cypress* (WLB-210), the Gulf of Mexico's only seagoing buoy tender. He responded to Hurricanes Ike and Gustav and multiple tropical storms, as well as served as an on-scene skimming asset during the Deepwater Horizon oil spill response.

Batchelder attended the Eisenhower Leadership Development Program, a leadership development program conducted through the U.S. Military Academy at West Point and Columbia University, and earned a master's degree in social-organizational psychology from Columbia University in May 2011.

From 2011 to 2014, Batchelder was assigned to the Coast Guard Academy, serving as Foxtrot's company officer overseeing 120 cadets. During his final year, he served as the regimental and senior company officer working with cadet leadership, managing logistics for the Corps of Cadets and managing the Cadet Division's finance.

The affable officer served as the executive officer onboard *Juniper*, homeported in Newport, from 2014 to 2016. Responsible for the critical waterways of New York, New Jersey and Long Island Sound, *Juniper* ensured the busy waterways remained open during historically cold winters impacting critical aids to navigation.

From 2016 to 2018, Batchelder reported to Joint Task Force–East as the finance and administration branch director. He directed the finance and administrative needs of a seventy-one-member Department of Homeland Security interagency task force charged with carrying out the Southern Border and Approach Campaign to secure the southern maritime border.

In 2018, he was back on the *Juniper* and in command.

Batchelder said, "I like buoy tenders, and I like going on missions. The people I work with in the Coast Guard are good folks, and the service does a good job in training personnel to do their jobs. I like coming to work; I feel we are having a positive impact."

Chapter 17

A SURFMAN IN NEWBURYPORT REMEMBERS A TRAINEE FLIPPING A FORTY-SEVEN-FOOTER

One of the selling points of the Coast Guard's forty-seven-foot motor lifeboat is that if it flips over in high seas, it will right itself in less than ten seconds. Patrick Brown, until recently officer in charge of Coast Guard Station Merrimack River in Newburyport, Massachusetts, has found this to be true.

"I was training a Coastie in Oregon, where the seas can get rough," said Brown, a native of Milford, New Hampshire. "He was at the helm, an error was made and we went over. But we came up again. Everyone was strapped in, no one was lost, no one was injured and the engine was still running. Our training had worked, in that everyone did what they were supposed to do."

Brown stated that it was a very awkward trip back to port. "He felt badly," Brown said.

At Newburyport, he supervised the activities of about twenty-six people who are ready to hit the surf at the first sound of a panicky boater.

The number of pleasure boats in the community, located at the juncture of the Merrimack River and the Atlantic Ocean, has grown in recent years. There are about 1,500 pleasure vessels on the Newburyport side of the Merrimack and about 500 on the Salisbury and Amesbury shores.

The Coast Guard, which was founded in Newburyport, makes many friends during a boating season. A message on the station's blog by a boater named Tom Perry said, "I want to extend my thanks to CG Station Merrimack, and in particular the crew, for your vigilance yesterday at the mouth of the river.

Patrick Brown was the officer in charge of Station Merrimack in Newburyport, Massachusetts, and holds the coveted classification of surfman. *Bryan Eaton photo, courtesy of the* Daily News, *Newburyport.*

"Although [the boat] 'Duet' didn't require assistance, the conditions were pretty bad, and it was nice to know you were on top of the situation and right with us at the end of our 30-plus hour trip. I wish all of our tax money was so well spent."

Brown holds the rank of senior chief, petty officer.

He joined the service in early 2000 and has been posted in communities including Barnegat Light, New Jersey; Coos Bay, Oregon; Port Allerton Station (Hull), Massachusetts; and Station Marquette, Michigan (Lake Superior).

He said that one of the biggest changes in the Coast Guard since his arrival is that its role in national security has increased. "After September 11, we began thinking Homeland Security," said the soft-spoken Brown. "We were told to board more ships and boats and to really be looking at crews and cargoes. In the Boston area, that was particularly true because ship traffic is much higher."

Also, a terminal that services tankers carrying liquid nitrogen is located near Charlestown, a community adjacent to Boston.

Brown holds the distinction of having qualified as a surfman, meaning he is highly skilled and can take the helm in heavy weather, including fifty-knot winds with twenty-foot seas. "The qualification means that you have been evaluated to make good judgments while operating in an extreme environment," said Brown.

Brown said he got into the Coast Guard to help people, as many Coasties do. In recent years, much of his satisfaction comes from training. "I enjoy working with new personnel, helping them learn and watching them rise in capability," said Brown.

Though Coast Guard teams here go out frequently for training on the water, service personnel are always working to be prepared. "There is a routine here: we train, we maintain and we operate," Brown said. "We're always working to get better at what we do.

"We get new personnel regularly. Some might be recruits, others might have a few years of experience. There are different levels of skills. Training is very important so we know that everyone can do the job."

Newburyport is one of about two dozen Coast Guard cities in the United States. Brown said, "It's clear Newburyport really supports the Coast Guard. We appreciate that."

Chapter 18

COMMANDER MIXES CAREER AND FAMILY, FROM NEW ORLEANS TO BOSTON

M any Coast Guard women face challenges when it comes to starting a family. Commander Kelly Denning, a 1998 graduate of the Coast Guard Academy, faced her difficult moment by taking two years off. The service has a program that permits members to take a two-year temporary separation. It enabled her and her Coast Guard husband to get organized and begin a life with children.

Today, she and her husband, Commander Matthew Denning (prevention department head at Sector Boston), have three children, James, Thomas and Mercie.

"I enjoyed the break, and I am very happy I came back in," said Denning, recently based in Boston. "Growing up, we were a military family, and my mother was an Army wife. The Coast Guard was good. They said if you want to take time off, do it. I enjoy my career; I love my family. I am glad I was able to leave and then come back."

One attribute of many Coast Guard women is that they are organized and skilled; they can advance in a career and start a family. And Denning has had a full career. Her first assignment after graduating from the Academy was onboard the USCGC *Confidence* out of Port Canaveral, Florida. She then traveled to Mobile to take command of the USCGC *Stingray*. She said that the Coast Guard mission for patrol boats changed drastically following the attacks of September 11, 2001.

Denning, who spent her formative years in Texas, went to New Orleans to be a command duty officer at the Eighth District Command Center (New

Orleans). She was also hurricane officer from 2002 to 2005 but was reassigned just before Katrina. During her time in New Orleans, Denning earned a master's degree in emergency and disaster management from Touro University International.

From 2005 to 2007, Denning was operations officer onboard the USCGC *Northland*, homeported out of Portsmouth, Virginia. She boarded the *Northland* to take her back to the New Orleans area for Hurricane Katrina relief. While there, she also responded in the aftermath of Hurricane Rita.

Following that, she reported to Training Center Yorktown, Virginia, as assistant search and rescue school chief. While there, she obtained her one-hundred-ton master's license.

Commander Kelly Denning has served at numerous stations, including here in Boston. *Dyke Hendrickson photo.*

And then came her voluntary separation. From 2008 to 2010, Denning took the temporary separation to take care of her newborn son and have another son. During that time, she affiliated with the reserves and drilled one year at Sector Hampton Roads Command Center and another year at Sector Puget Sound Command Center.

She returned to active duty in 2010 to take the operational planner (DXO) position at the Thirteenth Coast Guard District for three years, where she oversaw the Standard Operational Planning Process. She planned and executed several full-scale exercises with both the U.S. and Canadian navies while also completing the Master Exercise Practitioner Program and having a daughter.

Next, she went back to New Orleans to be the sector enforcement chief for two years and then "fleeted up" to take the response department head job for two years. She is currently stationed at the First District as deputy of incident management and lives in Medford, Massachusetts.

"The Coast Guard Academy was the only college I applied to," Denning said. "I thought about the Air Force Academy, but my eyes weren't good enough."

She said she talked with a friend in the Coast Guard and they discussed a career on sea rather than on land. "He said if you want to drive boats, you might want the Coast Guard. I thought that's what I wanted to do, and it's the only college I applied to."

While she was in New London, she helped start a competitive swim team. Prior to her arrival, the Academy did not offer a women's swimming team.

With almost two decades of active duty, she said, "I've enjoyed trips to sea and being on land. Generally, the camaraderie is really the best, and there are a lot of opportunities."

On merging a career with a family, she said, "My thought is be true to yourself. Identify what you value and pursue those goals. I have done that in the Coast Guard, and I am very happy with the way it has turned out."

Chapter 19

MASTER CHIEF MENTORS
IN CONNECTICUT

Master Chief Jay Galazin was late to the Coast Guard, but he made a rapid ascent once he finally enlisted.

"I joined when I was twenty-seven," said Galazin, a highly decorated service member who was serving as an instructor of leadership skills at the Coast Guard Academy in New London in the summer of 2018. "I had grown up in Simi Valley, California, and there were a lot of police, firefighters and other first responders in my neighborhood.

"I wanted to go in the direction of public service because I get a lot of satisfaction from helping people. When I finally joined, I really liked it. I wish I had enlisted earlier."

His early vocations included construction and restaurant work.

The well-traveled Coastie has been to numerous postings, including Iraq. Galazin, who once fished in the Santa Barbara Channel in Southern California, found himself inspecting many small fishing vessels captained by hardworking Iraqis.

"Off the coast of Iraq," Galazin said, "Coast Guard ships are busy checking fishing boats and tankers to make sure terrorists are not lurking. We board boats from thirty-foot fishing vessels to cargo vessels with huge containers.

"Fishermen are like farmers, hoping to make money from a natural asset. They are earnest; they want freedom like everyone else."

Galazin has developed a successful career in the Coast Guard, moving from a humble enlistee to serving as officer in charge of small vessels. Holding the rank of master chief petty officer is considered a major achievement.

Some Coast Guard personnel get a late start but advance rapidly, as was the case of Jay Galazin, shown here during a teaching stint in New London, Connecticut. *Dyke Hendrickson photo.*

In the summer of 2018, he was a teacher at the Leadership Development Center in New London. His title was school chief, Boat Forces Command Cadre. His primary responsibility was to provide leadership training and support for new and returning Boat Forces Commands. Prior to that, he was officer in charge for USCGC *Blacktip* in Channel Islands, California.

The Coast Guard stresses training, and the Leadership Development Center offers more than twenty leadership courses to more than five thousand officers and enlisted, reservist and civilian Coast Guard personnel annually. It also offers technical skills training to members assigned to positions aboard cutters, small boat stations and marine safety security teams. Training occurs at sites including New London; Petaluma, California; and Yorktown, Virginia.

Galazin's past postings include officer in charge of CG Station Toledo, executive petty officer of CG Station New Orleans and executive petty officer of the CGC *Blackfin* in Santa Barbara. Other assignments were on the cutters *Sturgeon* and *Point Sal* and as a coxswain at Station Noyo River. Galazin started his career on the CGC *Nantucket* in Key West.

"I like teaching and mentoring," he said. "I joined late but have enjoyed the many roles I have had in the Coast Guard."

Galazin's personal awards include the Meritorious Service Medal with Operational Distinguishing Device, three Coast Guard Commendation Medals with Operational Distinguishing Device, two Coast Guard Achievement Medals with Operational Distinguishing Device, the Iraqi Campaign Medal and several others. He has both the enlisted command ashore and afloat pins. He is designated a permanent cutterman, as well as having received his Advanced Boat Forces pin and his Coxswain pin.

He (lightheartedly) said his motto is, "When caught between the Devil and the Deep Blue Sea, start caulking the seam."

Chapter 20

VETERAN IN MAINE RETELLS FAMILY STORY ABOUT RESCUE AT SEA DURING CIVIL WAR

Mark Colby comes from a long line of ship captains in Newburyport, Massachusetts, the birthplace of the Coast Guard. He himself served four years (1969–73). Perhaps because he spent time in the service—mostly on the icebreaker *North Wind*—he pursued a life on the water after he left the service.

He earned a Coast Guard Merchant Mariner's license in both sail and power. He has been in the boat delivery field, and the soft-spoken veteran served as captain for private yachts. He's even piloted a vessel in Maine that took tourists to hidden coves and harbors to view the colorful puffins.

Retired now in Boothbay Harbor, Maine, he brought many of his interests together in a book about his grandfather that he published in 2013, *William Johnson Colby: A Remarkable Life Remembered, 1887–1951.*

"I enjoyed the Coast Guard," said Colby, who even today flies a Coast Guard flag on his front porch. "I had one year of college at University of Maine, Portland-Gorham, and then I left. The Vietnam War was going on. My brother had joined the Navy, but I didn't want to follow in his footsteps.

"I would not have shrunk away from Vietnam; I was ready to do my duty. But the Coast Guard offered adventure, travel and the chance to save lives. I had grown up near the water in New England, and the Coast Guard was a good choice at the time."

Colby was a bright recruit and qualified as a radio officer third class. He went to Cape May for basic training and then spent close to six months on Governor's Island, New York, learning Morse code. He opted for the Thirteenth District, focusing on Washington and Oregon, and found himself on an icebreaker, *North Wind*, out of Nome, Alaska. The icebreaker had about 180 men (there were just men then), and cruises included two to the Arctic and one to Antarctica. On one trip in the Bering Sea, his vessel rescued a pair who had gone down in their chopper.

"It felt good to be of help to these two," said Colby. "My reasons for entering the service included helping people and saving lives. This rescue was satisfying."

In Antarctica, the *North Wind* was once slowed by the ice. Officers were considering radioing for choppers to take the crew out. "As radio operator, I would have been left behind with a skeletal crew at first," said Colby. "That sounded like it would be an awkward moment for me.

"But the wind shifted, the current changed direction and the *North Wind* was able to free itself. Overall, things went pretty well for me in the Coast Guard, and after service, I returned to college."

He eventually got a master's degree in educational administration. For several years, he served as teacher-director of an eight-pupil school off Cuttyhunk Island, Massachusetts. Colby was also dedicated to raising his three children after his divorce.

A lover of history, Colby published *William Johnson Colby: A Remarkable Life Remembered, 1887–1951*. William Johnson Colby was an educator, a boater and a family man.

The Colby family, based in Newburyport, Massachusetts, was one of the most illustrious in the community in producing remarkable mariners. Mark Colby includes numerous anecdotes in the 130-page illustrated book. Here is an excerpt from a chapter titled "Captain Isaac N. Colby's Account of the Burning of the *Sonora* and *Highlander* in 1863." This selection is included because it is a "New England story." It also suggests that life on the high seas, then as now, could be dangerous and unpredictable.

Isaac Colby provides a self-portrait starting from birth in Newburyport on February 28, 1838. He started his life at sea at sixteen and worked his way up the ladder, including eighteen years with the Cushing family of Newburyport, "with an additional 20 or so years as master/owner of the *H.G. Johnson*."

Isaac's account focuses on his role as chief mate. Isaac Newton Colby was Mark Colby's great-grandfather.

It discusses the *Sonora*, a Newburyport ship, that traveled to distant cities like Melbourne and Calcutta. Seamen today study celestial navigation much like mariners of two centuries ago did.

Mark Colby comes from a family of ship captains, and he wrote a book about the daring seafaring exploits of some distant relatives. *Photo from collection of Mark Colby.*

Here is the recollection of Isaac Colby, who served as top mate on the *Sonora* in 1863, the year it was boarded and burned by the *Alabama*, a dreaded Confederate vessel. The text notes that the *Alabama* was a steam-driven vessel and had no trouble approaching ships of sail that were becalmed.

"In March 1863, I was chief mate of the American ship *Sonora*. The *Sonora* was at Pier 10 East River, N.Y., loading in the berths for Melbourne, Australia. At this time, the Confederate cruiser *Alabama* was the terror of the seas, burning fine ships in distant places.

"Our cargo was what we call general, consisting of a miscellaneous assortment of Yankee notions. We were in good sailing trim as space was reserved 'between decks' for steerage passengers, of whom we carried 40; we also had four cabin passengers. Most of these were leaving the country for fear of being drafted into the army.

"The ship reached Melbourne about July 2, and passengers departed. The ship then took on 212 Chinese passengers for Hong Kong. They delivered their passengers and took on a new group for Singapore. We arrived at Singapore on Dec. 11."

Though American seamen talked of the *Alabama*, at first no destruction was reported in nearby waters.

"We were bound for the Bay of Bengal. The American ship *Highlander* sailed in company, bound for the same port. I was standing on the forecastle with the crew, ready to lift our anchor as soon as the breeze came near, when the boatswain, a stalwart Negro, said excitedly, 'Good Lord! That is the *Alabama*!'

"We were helpless to resist and could not run away (we were becalmed), so we had to reconcile ourselves to the idea of leaving our beautiful ship that had been our home for nine months. What made the situation even more grievous was that the boarding office and the entire boat's crew were Englishmen. We were at war with the Confederacy and were prepared to accept the fortune of war, but it was a bitter pill to swallow when it was offered by British hands, manning a British ship, armed with British guns."

After some cool discussion, the invading captain "told me it was necessary to lower our two quarter boats, and for all the crew to proceed alongside the *Alabama*. We could take a bag of clothing but no trunks, no nautical instruments, books or charts.

"The British officer remained on board. The captain went away in the steamer's boat. I took the second mate and three men in a small boat and the remainder of the crew took another boat, and we all pulled to the steamer. The captain only was allowed to board. Shortly afterwards he came to the side near the mizzen rigging, where my boat was lying. The officer said to the crew, 'Never mind the papers; see if there is any money there.'

"But he found no money for the captain had entrusted it to me and it was rolled up in my stockings at the bottom of the bag. Seems they gave our Capt. Brown the choice of staying on board the *Alabama*, and be landed when and where the most convenient, or be set adrift in the sea with no water.

"He chose the latter and coming into my boat, the painter was cast off and we were left to ourselves, with no water or food of any kind. We were miles away from the nearest land, which was an inhospitable coast covered with jungle and infested with tigers.

"The tide had turned, and we were quite a distance from the ship. The *Alabama* steamed off to the *Highlander* and the same result followed, that is, the capture of the ship and the removal of the crew.

"We were getting farther and farther away from the *Sonora* and we saw the flames rise and envelope the hulls, the sails and the spars. It was a sad sight for we had got to love the ship, as it was our home, it furnished employment."

The crews of the *Sonora* and *Highlander* met and shared food.

"I was eventually glad to accept the offer of the captain of a passing British steamer to take passage with him to Singapore. On our way we passed over or near the spot where the *Sonora* burned to the water's edge and sunk at her anchors. We could not see her, of course, but I thought of the charred wreck of the once lofty and proud ship that carried the flag over so many years.

"In a few days we arrived at Singapore, where I found a portion of our crew that were in the first boat from the *Sonora*. They had a sad tale which included the sinking of the *Highlander*.

"It was here I found all the late crew of the *Sonora* with the exception of Captain Brown and the second mate, who had gone to Calcutta. I remained there until the 11th of February 1864, when I took passage for Boston in the American bark, *Pearl*. I arrived the 20th of June in Newburyport, nearly 15 months after leaving New York."

Chapter 21

RETIRED CAPTAIN HEADS ALUMNI ASSOCIATION AFTER STARTING FAMILY IN CONNECTICUT

A ndrea Marcille, in her notable career, advanced to the rank of captain, which means she was a capable officer who made good decisions. And in terms of postings, she rose to be the executive officer of the *Eagle*, the 295-foot tall ship that the Coast Guard maintains and sails. She has also served as commanding officer of the Leadership and Cadet Training Center at the Coast Guard Academy.

And later in life, at the age of forty-two, she decided to start a family. She and her husband now have a son.

Marcille is a native of New London, the home of the Coast Guard Academy. Now retired from the Coast Guard, she is executive of the Coast Guard Alumni Association, based on the Coast Guard campus. It is a nonprofit organization that provides services for and promotes fellowship among its members. Its primary purpose is to raise funds that provide a margin of excellence for the Academy and the Corps of Cadets. Most Coast Guard observers would view it as a plum job.

In an age when some women ask if they can "have it all," Marcille appears to be steaming ahead on her own course and speed.

The friendly leader had a big career before heading the alumni association. Marcille graduated from the Coast Guard Academy in 1991. Her resume includes the following chronology: USCGC *Decisive*, St. Petersburg, 1989–1991, deck watch officer; Training Center Yorktown, 1991–94, Maritime Law Enforcement School instructor; USCGC *Chase*, Long Beach, 1994–96, operations officer; USCGC *Pea Island*, Mayport, Florida, 1996–98,

Andrea Marcille, who once was a top officer on the *Eagle*, now heads the Coast Guard Academy Alumni Association in New London. *Dyke Hendrickson photo.*

commanding officer; Indiana University, Bloomington, 1998–99, MS in instructional systems technology; Training Center Cape May, 1999–2003, chief, Performance Technology Branch; USCGC *Eagle*, New London, 2003–5, executive officer; U.S. Coast Guard Academy, New London, 2005–10, cadet training officer; Leadership Development Center, New London, 2010–14, commanding officer.

She said one of her dilemmas as she reached the apex of her career was choosing between commanding a ship and becoming a mother. If she went to sea on a major Coast Guard cutter for two years for her next assignment, she would be a strong candidate for a job considered one of the best in the service: commanding the *Eagle* and training the next generation of Coast Guard officers who sail aboard the ship. Marcille was the first woman to serve as the executive officer on the New London–based ship, and many within the Coast Guard predicted she would be *Eagle*'s first female commander. But she chose family after more than two decades of devotion to the Coast Guard.

"I realized I didn't want to be defined in my life just by being a successful Coast Guard officer," Marcille said during an interview in the summer of 2018.

"I had a fulfilling career and I wanted to do more, in terms of a family. We are so pleased with our son and how much he adds to our life, our family. It was the right decision. One of the greatest gifts is to be able to pass on what you've learned in life to someone else, to your children. I wanted that opportunity."

Marcille didn't go out to sea. She started a family, and a son, Alex, is the product.

When Alex is older, Marcille said she will tell him how much the Coast Guard has meant to her and her husband, Nicholas Mynuk. Mynuk retired from the Coast Guard in 2008.

"When I look at Alex, it seems comical that it was even a hard decision for me," she said. "It's the right decision in so many ways. But when anyone is at a crossroads, you can't see what is beyond the curves so it's hard to know what's the right path to take."

After many years, Marcille said she has found a balance between her job and her family. She said she's very grateful to her family for supporting her earlier in her career while she struggled to find that balance.

She said, "Young women who come into the Coast Guard might want to have a family and yet they feel compelled to be very career-focused. It's about finding the right balance, and everyone is on that journey to figure out what a successful life is for them."

Marcille said her advice is, "Don't let someone else dictate what success means for you. It has to be your own path. I'd hate for someone to look back on a life or on a career and not to have it meant everything to them."

Chapter 22

AUXILIARY, TYPIFIED BY JOE AMORE, IS A POWERFUL FORCE THAT SUPPORTS COAST GUARD

Joe Amore is a member of the Coast Guard Auxiliary and a staff officer in public education of the service's First Northern Region, Division Three, on the North Shore of Massachusetts. He is a businessman—a small-company owner. He did not serve in the military service. But he puts in numerous hours per year in carrying out tasks that support the Coast Guard at outposts such as Station Merrimack River in Newburyport, Massachusetts. Amore is like many Auxiliary members who provide for the common good.

One task he carries out is public education. He teaches classes in boating safety at the Newburyport Adult and Community Education School in Newburyport. In most New England states, power-boat owners must be licensed. Amore teaches courses that enable newcomers to learn about safety, navigation and weather conditions. At the least, those who pass his course qualify for better insurance rates. And they learn about the difficult conditions at the mouth of the Merrimack River.

Safety is a priority for the Coast Guard, the Auxiliary and the Reserve. They stress that life belts should always be worn. Indeed, I observed a thirty-six-foot motor vessel in Norwalk, Connecticut, heading into Long Island Sound. I was surprised to note that all six passengers on the craft were wearing flotation devices. I knew it was a good practice to wear these belts, but I had rarely seen each passenger on a boat equipped with a preserver. And then I realized it was a team of Auxiliary members going out for a cruise that could include the inspection of boats.

Auxiliarists are authorized to board pleasure craft to inspect them for fitness. Does the boat carry a life preserver for each passenger? Are there fire extinguishers aboard? Is the vessel fit for the water? Auxiliary members can send a vessel back to the dock if too many passengers are on board.

"It's the law that there has to be a preserver for each person on board," said Amore, who also teaches boating basics for new owners. "And they should be worn. People fall off vessels at the dock or on a cruise itself. You never know.

"Hypothermia is a big problem in New England. The water is so cold that it can affect someone who goes overboard, even if they are a good swimmer. The blood leaves the head, so decision-making can be impaired. The upper chest gets numb. The hands get

Joe Amore, a safety teacher and boating coach, has been a major force in the Coast Guard Auxiliary on the North Shore of Massachusetts. *Dyke Hendrickson photo.*

numb, too, and can be hard to manage. Sometimes a boater who goes into the water can't grab a ladder or control a lifeline because the hands aren't responding."

Amore said that hypothermia can be a killer. He recalled that several years ago, a father and son went overboard in the Atlantic near the mouth of the Merrimack River in Massachusetts. "Rescuers got to them, but hypothermia played a role in the teen's death. He was about fifteen, and he was thin and wiry. His father was very heavy, and his body fat helped in warding off the cold.

"Both were pulled out of the water and rushed to shore. The teenager died. His father lived. Temperature in New England water is especially cold in early spring or late autumn."

The United States Coast Guard Auxiliary is a uniformed unpaid complement of the Coast Guard. It was established in 1939, in part to help supervise the growing number of recreational boaters. Coast Guard officials say the Auxiliary exists to support USCG missions except in roles that require direct law enforcement or military engagement.

Rhode Island Lieutenant Governor Dan McKee, *left*, speaks with officers Kurt Virkaitis and Brian McSorley, following an event recognizing Coast Guard Auxiliary Day at the State Capitol Building. *U.S. Coast Guard photo by Petty Officer Third Class Zachary Hupp.*

Coast Guard Petty Officer First Class Gregg Woodworth, *left*, shows Maine students how to load and discharge a flare gun. The Coast Guard teaches basic boating skills, including navigation, communication and knot tying. *U.S. Coast Guard photo by Petty Officer Second Class Etta Smith.*

Coast Guard Captain Richard Schultz, sector commander of Sector Southeastern New England, *right*, presents Jack Cowley with a challenge coin from the First Coast Guard district admiral in Woods Hole, Massachusetts. Cowley retired from the Coast Guard Auxiliary after close to twenty years of service. *U.S. Coast Guard photo by Commander Jeannot Smith.*

As of 2018, there were approximately twenty-four thousand members of the U.S. Coast Guard Auxiliary.

The Auxiliary differs from the Coast Guard Reserve in that Auxiliary members are unpaid. They get expenses. For instance, if they are using their own boats on the water, they can get reimbursed for gas and oil. Reserve members are salaried and have monthly obligations. Because they are "contracted" to the Coast Guard, they can be called up for active duty.

The Coast Guard Reservist normally trains two days a month and may perform up to fifteen days of active duty for training a year. The Coast Guard Reserve has about eight thousand men and women in service nationally, most of them integrated directly with regular Coast Guard units.

Nationally, the Auxiliary is much larger, and it contributes over 4.5 million hours of service each year and completes nearly 500,000 missions in service to support the Coast Guard. Every year, Auxiliarists help to save approximately 500 lives, assist 15,000 distressed boaters, conduct over 150,000 safety examinations of recreational vessels and provide boater safety instruction to over 500,000 students.

In 2003, the Coast Guard, Coast Guard Reserve and Coast Guard Auxiliary were realigned under the Department of Homeland Security.

Those in the Auxiliary today board vessels to check for excessive use of alcohol or drugs. Anecdotal evidence suggests that drunkenness is the cause of many mishaps on New England water. In recent years, the use of opioids has emerged as a problem among commercial fishermen.

Auxiliarists also attempt to supervise traffic. They urge boaters to travel slowly to avoid creating wakes. Also, captains must observe navigation aids that populate most New England waters. In some areas, the tides can make for unexpected groundings. In rivers or shallow harbors leading to the Atlantic, sandbars can move from year to year. "Stay to the right and be observant," said Amore. "Have respect for other boaters. Go slowly in narrow spaces to keep down the wake."

Another task that most Auxiliaries undertake is hosting an open house at the local Coast Guard station. When properly publicized, the open house can draw hundreds. Parents and grandparents bring youngsters, who can walk around the Coast Guard vessel (with supervision). A forty-seven-foot rescue vessel can handle more than a dozen at a time. Inevitably, there are long lines at the annual events.

The Auxiliary undertakes such duties as harbor control and education courses with the goal of freeing full-time Coast Guard personnel for other tasks. Since 2003, when the Coast Guard was melded into the Department of Homeland Security, its full-time members spend more time on potential danger and fewer hours supervising recreational boating.

If a pleasure craft contacts the Coast Guard station with an "emergency" such as running out of gas or losing a rudder, they might check out the situation before passing it to a private concern such as TowBoatUSA. If they are called to a significant offshore emergency, the station chief might direct some Auxiliary members to man the communications station while they go out in rescue boats. Those in the Auxiliary have to qualify for each role they volunteer to carry out. Training sessions are held throughout New England to enable new volunteers to play larger roles in the Auxiliary.

There are about 2,300 members of the Auxiliary in the First Northern District, New England. This includes Maine, New Hampshire, Massachusetts and Rhode Island. Teams are organized in dozens of flotillas, which can be found on lakes and rivers as well as the Atlantic.

Auxiliary officials say that in a given year in New England, the Auxiliary completes 3,000 operational patrols, conducts 1,800 boating-safety classes, conducts 5,000 vessel safety checks, conducts 300 commercial fishing inspections and assists 130 persons in peril. Flotilla members conduct 1,200 visits to marine dealers to distribute safety literature. And members provide more than 130,000 hours of volunteer support to the Coast Guard, officials say.

"I think we are a valuable part of the Coast Guard," said Amore, who has been active for close to twenty years. "We do tasks that permit the active members to respond to emergencies and provide security along coasts and waterfronts.

"Auxiliary members are trained. They are capable. They provide education and training to thousands who enjoy New England boating. And in my years with the organization, I have never encountered boaters who have objected to our presence."

Chapter 23

NEW ENGLAND PLAYED KEY ROLE IN HISTORY OF THE COAST GUARD

T he Coast Guard has a long and meritorious history, starting in New England and stretching over the globe. The following is a portion of that history, taken from Coast Guard documents. An overview of the service would include the fact that the modern Coast Guard is the product of at least three other agencies.

The Revenue Marine Service merged with the Life-Saving Service in 1915, and the term "U.S. Coast Guard" was formally ascribed to the organization. In 1939, the Lighthouse Service was folded into the Coast Guard.

Some of the most significant events had their origin in New England. That would include the birth of the Coast Guard in Newburyport in 1790; the development of the Sikorsky helicopters (to be used by the Coast Guard) in Stratford, Connecticut, in the early '40s; and the advent of women arriving at the Coast Guard Academy in New London in 1976.

The following are key dates in Coast Guard history. The events listed have roots in services that were independent until 1915. Some developments noted here occurred outside New England, but they are included because they add to the understanding of the early days of the service.

This listing comes from a history developed by Coast Guard historians. Some interpretation has been added by author Dyke Hendrickson.

1716: First lighthouse is built at Little Brewster Island, Boston.
1789, 7 August: An act of Congress, the first to make any provisions for public works, creates the Lighthouse Establishment, when it accepted title to and joined jurisdiction over the twelve lighthouses then in existence

Alexander Hamilton is known as the Father of the Coast Guard because of his work to create the Revenue Cutter Service in 1790. *U.S. Coast Guard photo.*

and provided that "the necessary support, maintenance and repairs of all lighthouses, beacons, buoys and public piers erected, placed, or sunk before the passing of this act, at the entrance of, or within any bay, inlet, harbor, or port of the United States, for rendering the navigation thereof easy and safe, shall be defrayed out of the treasury of the United States." Prior to this time, the lighthouses had been paid for, built and administered first by the colonies and then the states.

1790, 4 August: Congress authorizes Secretary of the Treasury Alexander Hamilton's proposal to build ten cutters to protect the new nation's revenue. Alternately known as the system of cutters, Revenue Service and Revenue-Marine, this service would officially be named in 1863. The cutters were placed under the control of the Treasury, as the Revenue Cutter Service Department. This date is the officially recognized birthday of the Coast Guard.

1791: The cutter *Massachusetts* is commissioned at Newburyport, Massachusetts. She is thought to be the first ship constructed by the service, and it is largely for this reason that Newburyport is known as the birthplace of the Coast Guard. That claim was confirmed in writing by President Lyndon Johnson in 1965. A marine cutter had four officers, four enlisted men and two cabin boys. It was armed with about six small cannons. The *Massachusetts* was about sixty feet long.

1794, 5 June: The Third Congress authorizes an additional ten revenue cutters and gave the Treasury Department responsibility for lighthouses, beacons, buoys and piers.

1798: Hostilities begin in the Quasi-War with France. The revenue cutters *Pickering, Virginia, Scammel, South Carolina, Governor Jay, Eagle, General Greene* and *Diligence* were the first to be placed under naval orders, composing about one-third of the U.S. fleet. Unaided revenue cutters took eighteen of the twenty-two vessels captured by the United States between 1798 and 1799.

1799, 25 February: The service becomes responsible for enforcing quarantine laws at sea. The Revenue Cutter Service was charged with enforcing the unpopular law, which hampered trade in New England ports. The act was eventually repealed but contributed to the outbreak of war.

1808, 1 January: Law making the slave trade from Africa illegal goes into effect. Revenue cutters were charged with enforcing this law. However, New England shipyards still built vessels for slaving operations owned by companies in other countries.

1812, 18 June: The United States declares war on Great Britain.

1815, 18 February: Treaty of Ghent ends hostilities between the United States and Great Britain.

1821: Augustin Jean Fresnel develops the Fresnel lens, utilizing the refractive properties of glass to magnify light beams. This technology was used for years in New England shoreline lighthouses.

1822, 23 February: Passage of the Timber Act. Congress creates a ship timber reserve for the U.S. Navy and authorizes the president to use whatever forces necessary to prevent the cutting of live oak on public lands. This task suited the shallow-draft revenue cutters, and they were used extensively. This marks the start of the service's environmental mission.

1830, 7 December: President Andrew Jackson introduces a plan to add a large number of lighthouses to the federal system, with a total of fifty-one more lighthouse keepers. He supports the practice of offsetting the costs of keeping aids to navigation on the coasts, lakes and harbors.

1831, December: Treasury secretary Louis McLane directs the revenue cutter *Gallatin* to cruise the coast in search of persons in distress. This is the first time a government agency is tasked specifically to search for those who might be in danger.

1843: Captain Alexander V. Fraser, Revenue Cutter Service, is appointed chief of the newly created Revenue Marine Bureau of Treasury and becomes the service's first commandant.

1845: Congress authorizes the first Revenue Cutter Service Engineering Corps in response to needs generated by steam engine technology. Metal buoys are first put into service. The riveted iron barrels replaced the older wooden stave construction.

1846: Almost a dozen cutters are assigned to cooperate with the Army and Navy in the Mexican War. Cutters *McLane, Legare, Woodbury, Ewing, Forward* and *Van Buren* are assigned to the Army. Cutters *Wolcott, Bibb, Morris* and *Polk* are assigned to the Navy. The Coast Guard has participated in every U.S. war.

1851, 17 April: Minot's Ledge Lighthouse in Scituate, Massachusetts, the first built in the United States exposed to the full force of the ocean, is swept away during a storm with the loss of two men. Assistant keepers Joseph Wilson and Joseph Antoine apparently maintained their station, ringing the lighthouse's bell, until waves swept the tower away.

1857: Construction begins on the *Harriet Lane*. The cutter is equipped with a steam engine and side paddle wheels and was considered the height of technology.

The Life-Saving Service merged with the Revenue Cutter Service in 1915 to create the modern Coast Guard. Here is a photo from 1892 that shows a crew rushing to save a ship off Plum Island, Massachusetts. *Courtesy Custom House Maritime Museum, Newburyport.*

1860: Fresnel lenses are in use at all U.S. lighthouses.

1861, 13 April: The revenue cutter *Harriet Lane* fires the first shot from a naval vessel in the Civil War when she fires across the bow of the merchant vessel *Nashville* after the latter attempted to enter Charleston Harbor without displaying the national flag.

1863: Congress passes an act allowing the president to appoint commissioned officers of the Revenue Cutter Service with advice and consent of the Senate. This act contained the first statutory use of the term "Revenue Cutter Service." Previous laws referred only to "revenue cutters."

1865, 21 April: Cutters are ordered to search all outbound vessels for the assassins of President Lincoln.

1871, 20 April: In response to public demand, Congress appropriates $200,000 for a lifesaving service under the Treasury Department. It authorizes the employment of crews of paid surfmen and the construction of new stations where needed. The department assigned Captain John Faunce to review the state of lifesaving in the United States. His report found the system in deplorable disrepair and in a state of near-complete unreadiness. Sumner Increase Kimball, a native of Maine, is appointed to lead the Revenue Marine Bureau.

1872: The *Metis*, after being struck by a coastal schooner off the coast of Watch Hill, Rhode Island, sinks with a heavy loss of life. But Life-Saving Service and lighthouse personnel, along with the cutter *Moccasin*, rescue the survivors. The rescue signified the growing interaction among the three services, which played a factor in their later mergers.

1876: Revenue Cutter School of Instruction (predecessor of the Coast Guard Academy) is founded.

1877: Training of the first class of revenue cutter cadets begins on the school-ship *Dobbin*, with nine cadets, three officers, one surgeon, six warrant officers and seventeen crewmen on board.

1881: Lime Rock Lighthouse (Rhode Island) keeper Ida Lewis becomes the first woman to be awarded a Gold Lifesaving Medal.

1884: Bureau of Navigation is formed under the Department of the Treasury.

1888, November: Point Allerton (Massachusetts) Life-Saving Station keeper Joshua James and his crew rescue thirteen people from the schooners *Gertrude Abbott* and *H.C. Higginson*. They were awarded the Gold Lifesaving Medal the following year.

1889, 10–12 September: The lifesaving crews near Rehoboth Beach (Massachusetts) stations assist twenty-two vessels and save 39 persons by surfboat and 155 by breeches buoy without the loss of a single life

1890, 31 August: Cutter *Wolcott* confiscates undeclared opium on board the steamer *George E. Starr.* It is the first recorded narcotics seizure, though only because the opium had not been declared, not because of anti-narcotic laws. The cutter *Bear*, captained by Michael Healy, transports the first reindeer from Siberia to Alaska. The domesticated reindeer were part of an experiment to improve the living conditions of the native population, suggesting that revenue-cutter personnel pursued environmental interests many years ago.

HISTORY OF THE COAST GUARD, PART II

This section continues with dates that highlight major events in Coast Guard history in New England. It was compiled by Coast Guard historians.

1901, August: To evaluate its use in lighthouse work, radio equipment is installed experimentally on Nantucket Lightship, Massachusetts.

1902, 17 March: All but one of the crew members of the Monomoy Life-Saving Station, Chatham, Massachusetts, perish during the attempted rescue of the wrecked coal barge *Wadena* during a terrible winter gale. The dead include the keeper of the station, Marshall N. Eldridge; six of his surfmen; and the crew of five from the barge. Eldridge told his men before they departed on the rescue, "We must go, there is a distress flag in the rigging." The sole survivor, Seth L. Ellis, was the number one surfman of the Monomoy station. He was awarded the Gold Lifesaving Medal.

1910: Revenue Cutter School of Instruction moves from Curtis Bay, Maryland, to Fort Trumbull in New London, Connecticut.

1910, 4 April: President Taft, though he summered in Beverly, Massachusetts, recommends abolishing the Revenue Cutter Service to cut expenses. His actions led to the eventual creation of the Coast Guard by merging the Revenue Cutter Service and the Life-Saving Service on January 28, 1915.

1912, 14 April: RMS *Titanic* collides with an iceberg off Newfoundland while sailing on her maiden voyage from Southampton to New York. She sank two hours later. There were 1,517 lost, including 103 women and 53

children, out of total passenger and crew of 2,207. The tragedy led to the creation of the International Ice Patrol.

1914, 7 February: Following the Convention for Safety at Sea in London, President Woodrow Wilson directs the Revenue Cutter Service to assume responsibility for the International Ice Patrol, a mission the Coast Guard performs to this day.

1915, 28 January: President Woodrow Wilson signs the bill merging the Life-Saving Service and the Revenue Cutter Service to establish the U.S. Coast Guard.

1920, 16 January: The Volstead Act, better known as Prohibition, goes into effect. Enforcement of the act fell to the Treasury Department; the "Rum War" dominates Coast Guard's missions until the act is repealed in 1933. The challenge to control rumrunning along thousands of coastal miles was one of the largest challenges that ever confronted the Coast Guard. Commercial fishermen and even some Coasties were tempted to cooperate with smugglers for fast money.

1923: The Coast Guard establishes an oceanographic unit at Harvard University, Cambridge, Massachusetts, charged with providing support and conducting research for the International Ice Patrol.

1924: 31 destroyers, 203 cabin cruisers and 100 smaller boats are acquired by the Coast Guard for the rum war. With appropriate personnel, the cost is approximately $14 million, the largest single increase in the history of the Coast Guard.

1933: The Twenty-First Amendment repeals Prohibition. The Coast Guard refocuses on other missions. The Coast Guard Academy moves from Fort Trumbull to its present campus in New London, Connecticut.

1934, 13 May: Lightship *Nantucket* (*LV-117*) is struck and sunk by the RMS *Olympia*.

1939, 1 July: U.S. Lighthouse Service is consolidated with the Coast Guard. Made in the interest of efficiency and economy, the plan integrates approximately 30,000 aids to navigation (including light vessels and lighthouses), 5,200 employees, 64 buoy tenders, 30 depots and 17 district offices.

1939, 5 September: Inventor Igor Sikorsky constructs the first functioning helicopter in Connecticut. Choppers later became a major force in search-and-rescue operations.

1940, January: The Ocean Station program is established under orders from President Franklin Roosevelt. The Coast Guard, in cooperation with the U.S. Weather Service, is given responsibility for its establishment

A Coast Guard MH-60 Jayhawk helicopter crew conducts landings on the deck of the destroyer USS *Momsen*. Proficiency in helicopter rescue techniques has enabled the Coast Guard to travel rapidly to help troubled mariners. *U.S. Coast Guard photo by Petty Officer Third Class Lauren Dean.*

and operation. The program was first known as the Atlantic Weather Observation Service and later as the Ocean Station weather program.

1941: Coast Guard Reserve becomes the Auxiliary. The first civilian women are hired to serve in secretarial and clerical positions.

1941, January: Successful test of the Sikorsky VS-300 (HNS-1) helicopter in Connecticut.

1941, November: Coast Guard is ordered to operate as part of the Navy. In December, Japan attacks Pearl Harbor. USCGC *Taney* serves as an antiaircraft vessel against enemy aircraft and performs harbor and antisubmarine patrols alongside the Navy.

1942, January: USCGC *Alexander Hamilton* is struck by a torpedo while on convoy duty and sinks off the coast of Iceland. Historians say twenty-six members of her crew perished in the attack.

1942, September: Congress establishes the Women's Coast Guard Reserves, known as SPARs, an acronym for "Semper Paratus—Always Ready." Lieutenant Commander Dorothy Stratton is transferred from the Navy to serve as the director of the SPARs. More than eleven thousand SPARs serve during World War II, many in New England. The program was largely demobilized after the war.

1944, June: Coast Guard cutters, Coast Guard–manned warships and landing craft participate in the landings at Normandy, France. Four Coast Guard–manned vessels are lost at Omaha Beach that day. Sixty cutters sailed in support of the invasion forces, acting as search-and-rescue craft for each of the landings. Several months later, cutters *Eastwind* and *Southwind* captured the Nazi weather and supply vessel *Externsteine* off the coast of Greenland after a brief firefight with no casualties. The Coast Guardsmen christened it USS *Eastbreeze* and placed a prize crew of thirty-seven men on board. After sailing with the Greenland Patrol for three weeks, *Eastbreeze* proceeded to Boston, where the Navy renamed her USS *Callao*.

1946, January: Control of the Coast Guard is transferred back to the Department of the Treasury.

1946, May: Coast Guard leaders commission the former *Horst Wessel* (built in prewar Germany) as the *Eagle*. It was a war "prize," and the Coast Guard sails her to the United States Coast Guard Academy, where she presently serves as a sail-training vessel. The vessel is often docked in New London.

1952: Tankers SS *Fort Mercer* and SS *Pendleton* break in half during a severe nor'easter off the coast of Cape Cod. Coast Guard vessels, aircraft and lifeboat stations, working under harsh winter conditions, rescue seventy persons from the foundering ships. Five Coast Guardsmen earn the Gold Lifesaving Medal, four earn the Silver Lifesaving Medal and fifteen earn the Coast Guard Commendation Medal. The rescue was hailed in the movie *The Finest Hours*.

1956, 10 May: Passage of the Small Passenger Vessel Act. This act, passed to halt an increase in small boat accidents, requires all vessels carrying more than six passengers for hire, regardless of size or propulsion, be inspected by a marine inspector of the Coast Guard and meet safety standards. These standards included lifesaving and firefighting equipment, machinery and electrical installations, hull strength and stability considerations. This law also requires that the Coast Guard license operators.

1956, 25 July: The Swedish liner *Stockholm* collides with the Italian liner *Andrea Doria* off Nantucket, Massachusetts. Coast Guard cutters and aircraft, as well as other vessels, respond. The *Andrea Doria* sinks ten hours after the collision that resulted in fifty-two deaths

1961: Coast Guard establishes Cuban patrols to aid refugees and to enforce neutrality, interdicting the transportation of men and arms.

1961, March: Coast Guard leadership contracts for a new logo design that would become known as the "racing stripe," a narrow blue bar and wide orange-red bar canted sixty-four degrees running from lower left to upper right. Coast Guard Commandant Edwin Roland approves the design on April 6, 1967.

1970: Water Quality Act increases Coast Guard jurisdiction over hazardous spills to include pollutants such as mercury, pesticides and explosives.

1971, 10 August: President Richard Nixon signs the Federal Boat Safety Act of 1971, considered to be the most significant legislation in the long history of federal action in this field.

1972: The Federal Water Pollution Control Act and the Ports and Waterways Safety Act establish cleanup and liability standards for spills and call for Coast Guard scrutiny of hazardous materials in vessel construction and design. It also institutes a national emergency contingency plan for oil spills. The Coast Guard establishes Marine Environmental Response (MER) units concerned primarily with pollution response. The Coast Guard Research and Development Center (RDC) is established at Avery Point in Groton, Connecticut. It is the only facility conducting research, testing and development of the tools necessary to allow the U.S. Coast Guard to fulfill its role to protect the United States and its coasts and waterways.

1976: The Fishery Conservation and Management Act establishes a two-hundred-mile zone, quadrupling the offshore fishing area controlled by

Coast Guard Petty Officer Second Class Joanna Adams, an aviation maintenance technician, conducts maintenance on an aircraft's auxiliary power unit combustion liner. *U.S. Coast Guard photo by Petty Officer First Class Charly Hengen.*

the United States. The Coast Guard is responsible for enforcing this law. Later that year, the Liberian tanker *Argo Merchant* is grounded off Nantucket carrying 7.3 million gallons of fuel oil. Cutters *Sherman, Vigilant, Spar* and *Bittersweet* are on scene, but deteriorating weather and heavy seas prevent removal of its cargo before the hull begins to buckle. The bow is wrenched from the hull, causing the largest oil spill in American waters at that time. The *Argo Merchant* accident and fourteen more tanker accidents in or near American waters over the next ten weeks caused great concern about tanker construction, leading to a large tanker safety movement.

1976: The first female cadets enter the Coast Guard Academy in New London, Connecticut.

1977: The Coast Guard conducts an experiment integrating women in crews of seagoing vessels. The cutters *Morgenthau* and *Gallatin* receive ten enlisted women and two female officers each. As when the Coast Guard set up its first racially integrated ships during World War II, the "mixed crews" settle into a working routine.

1977, 21 April: Cuban exodus at Mariel. The Coast Guard aids approximately 125,000 Cuban refugees. It is the largest Coast Guard operation ever undertaken in peacetime to that date.

1982, 7 January: Lieutenant Colleen A. Cain, the Coast Guard's first female helicopter pilot, dies when the HH-52 *CG-1420*, on which she was copilot, crashes into a mountainside while on a rescue mission east of Honolulu, Hawaii. The pilot, Lieutenant Commander H.W. Johnson, and air crewman D.L. Thompson also perish.

1984: Coast Guard Authorization Act is passed. The commandant of the Coast Guard shall use such sums as are necessary, from amounts appropriated for the operational maintenance of the Coast Guard, to establish a helicopter rescue swimmer program for the purpose of training selected Coast Guard personnel in rescue swimming skills.

1986, 28 January: The space shuttle *Challenger* explodes after liftoff, killing the entire crew, including a civilian teacher from New Hampshire. Coast Guard units, including the cutters *Dallas, Dauntless, Harriet Lane, Bear, Tampa, Cherokee, Sweetgum* and *Point Roberts*, conduct the initial search-and-rescue operations and later assist in the recovery of much of the shuttle's wreckage.

1986, 26 May: Kelly M. Mogk becomes the first woman to graduate from Navy Rescue Swimmer School and the first female Coast Guard rescue swimmer.

1990, March: The Oil Pollution Act is passed by Congress. The Coast Guard is tasked to assemble teams capable of a swift response to oil spills and other disasters. The act is the single largest law enforcement undertaking of the service since the passage of Prohibition.

1990, August: At the request of the joint chiefs of staff, the secretary of transportation and the commandant commit ten four-person Coast Guard law enforcement boarding teams (LEDET) to Operation Desert Shield. Approximately 60 percent of the six hundred boardings carried out by U.S. forces are either led or supported by a Coast Guard team.

1991, February: In response to oil spills caused by Iraqi burning wells and pumping stations, two HU-25A Falcon jets from Air Station Cape Cod deploy to Saudi Arabia as part of the interagency oil spill assessment team (USIAT). The jets carry Aireye technology, which locates and records oil as it floats on water. The Falcons map over forty thousand square miles in theater and locate "every drop of oil on the water...to produce a daily updated surface analysis of the location, condition, and drift projections of the oil."

1991, 6–10 October: NASA astronaut and Coast Guard Commander Bruce Melnick makes his first space flight when he serves as a mission specialist aboard the space shuttle *Discovery* on Space Shuttle Mission STS-41. *Discovery* deployed the Ulysses spacecraft for its five-year mission to explore the polar regions of the sun. Commander Melnick was the first Coast Guardsman selected by NASA for astronaut training. Melnick graduated from the Coast Guard Academy and spent a tour as a Coast Guard rescue pilot at the Cape Cod station before entering the astronaut program.

1991, 31 October: During an extremely severe winter storm, USCGC *Tamaroa* rescues four of five Air National Guard crewmen from an ANG H-60 that had ditched south of Long Island due to fuel exhaustion (the fifth crewman, a pararescue jumper, was never found). *Tamaroa* had been attempting to rescue the crew of the sailing vessel *Satori* the previous day when the cutter was diverted to assist the Air National Guard aircrew. *Tamaroa* was awarded the Coast Guard Unit Commendation. The events surrounding this storm off New England were chronicled in the book and movie *The Perfect Storm*, a film with roots in Gloucester.

1996, 1 October: Operation Frontier Shield becomes the largest counter-narcotics operation in Coast Guard history.

2000, 13 March: The Coast Guard announces the successful completion of Operation New Frontier. New Frontier evaluated the use of armed helicopters and high-speed small boats to stop small, high-speed vessels, referred to as "go-fasts," which smuggled narcotics to the United States.

Of the six go-fasts detected, all six were captured. Cutters *Gallatin* and *Seneca* took part in the evaluations.

2001, 11 September: Al Qaeda terrorists hijack four commercial U.S. aircraft, crashing two into the World Trade Center in New York City and one into the Pentagon in Washington, D.C. The fourth aircraft crashed around Shanksville, Pennsylvania, when passengers on board tried to regain control of the aircraft. The attacks killed over three thousand civilians. Coast Guard units, including Reservists and Auxiliarists in New England, were among the first military units to respond; they provided communications, security, evacuation by water and assistance to those in need.

2001, November: President George W. Bush establishes the Department of Homeland Security. This was the single largest reorganization of the federal government since the creation of the Department of Defense in 1947. This change expanded the role of the Coast Guard in New England.

2004, 24 April: Nathan Bruckenthal and two Navy sailors die when suicide bombers detonate the explosives on a boat they intercepted off the coast of Iraq. Bruckenthal was the first Coast Guard combat fatality since the Vietnam War. He had roots in Connecticut.

2005, August: Hurricane Katrina devastates the Gulf Coast. Many from New England are ordered to the area to help. The Coast Guard response includes 62 aircraft, 42 cutters, 131 small boats and over 5,000 Coast Guard personnel. By September 27, 2005, the Coast Guard had rescued 33,735 people.

2009, August: The Coast Guard has approximately 42,000 men and women on active duty, 7,500 Reservists, 30,000 Auxiliarists and 7,700 full-time civilian employees.

2012, October: The tall ship *Bounty* sinks off the coast of North Carolina after sailing from New London. It had been outfitted that fall in Boothbay Harbor, Maine. Coast Guard pilots and swimmers save fourteen of sixteen crew members and are honored for their efforts, which took place during Hurricane Sandy.

2015: The 791-foot tank *El Faro* goes down in heavy seas while carrying cargo to Puerto Rico. Coast Guard teams find wreckage, but all thirty-three crew members disappeared. The captain and a half dozen others were from Maine.

Chapter 24

A Rumrunner, a Foggy Night and the Death of a Coastie off Massachusetts during Prohibition

One of the key roles of the Coast Guard in the twentieth century was patrolling U.S. and international waters to interdict vessels smuggling illegal drugs. Coast Guard cutters travel the lower Atlantic and much of the Pacific in search of drug smugglers. The Coastie vessels are armed and dangerous.

Valuable technology can help identify vessels with contraband. In southern seas, small submarine-like "fast-boats" have been stopped and boarded. Tons of illegal drugs have been confiscated.

The federal government's pursuit of contraband is not new. During Prohibition (1920–33), government vessels from Maine to Key West, Florida, were on the alert for boats carrying beer, wine and whiskey. New England states were especially plagued by rumrunners, in part because the coastal states are close to foreign ports such as those in Canada.

Here is how it was put by author Everett S. Allen, who wrote *The Black Ships: Rumrunners of Prohibition* (Boston: Little, Brown and Co., 1965): "The Coast Guard was frequently, often painfully, reminded of the smugglers' successes and its own complex difficulties in attempting to combat a popular traffic whose entrepreneurs had money enough to buy whoever and whatever had to be bought, whose principals had the sympathy of perhaps every other man on the street, and whose militant activists shared the government's view that law enforcer and rumrunner were enemies and that this was war."

The following is a New England story by David Considine, BMCS, USCG (ret.), and Mark DuPont, CWO, USCG (ret.), that focuses on the Coast Guard battling the rumrunners years ago. It is an unfortunate tale because one Coast Guard member was killed by friendly fire.

HERE IS THE STORY: The crews at the Plum Island Coast Guard station and the crews from Base Seven in Gloucester were delegated the duty to patrol the shallow waters of Plum Island Sound and Ipswich Bay (Massachusetts) with smaller, more maneuverable vessels, while the larger picket boats remained a fair distance offshore. The Plum Island station would use its twenty-six-foot motor surfboat on nightly patrols to cover its portion of Plum Island Sound and Ipswich Bay. Coast Guard headquarters had received a letter issuing instructions on how Coast Guard vessels were to identify themselves while operating in support of the rum war. This letter was read to the Plum Island crews multiple times by Herman Schwartz BMC, the officer in charge of the Plum Island station. This letter included instruction on illuminating the CG ensign (the flag flown on all Coast Guard vessels as a means of identification) with a spotlight and instruction on the use of warning shots and disabling fire.

Monday, August 4, 1930, was a normal Monday at the Plum Island Coast Guard station, and the daily chores, training and boat work were finished early in anticipation of the night patrol. Boatswain Mate First Class Louis E. Pratt was the duty coxswain for the twenty-six-foot motor surfboat. Also on duty that day was Cleo Faulkingham, a twenty-two-year-old surfman, who had been in the Coast Guard for two years and four months. BMC Schwartz sent Pratt and Faulkingham to "guard the entrance to the Ipswich River."

Louis Pratt was from Burlington, Vermont, but had moved to Kittery, Maine, when he was sixteen. It was here he felt the call of the sea and decided to join the Coast Guard, enlisting at the Plum Island Coast Guard station on December 16, 1922. He served at the Plum Island station and left the service a year later, having fulfilled his yearlong commitment. He took two weeks off and then reenlisted, this time at the Portsmouth Harbor, New Hampshire station. Here he would stay three years until January 1927, when he was promoted to boatswain's mate first class. Following his promotion, he was transferred back to the Plum Island station. Pratt was married to Margaret Adams Pratt and was the father of a four-year-old daughter, both of whom lived in Kittery.

On August 4, Pratt and Faulkingham were issued two .45-caliber automatic pistols and ammunition. They usually would wait until 8:00 p.m. to depart for the patrol area, but on this night, they left at 7:30 p.m., as they had been told to drop a passenger off at Ipswich Bluffs. After leaving the passenger, they proceeded to Ipswich Neck Wharf, arriving a little after 8:00 p.m. After tying up, they were approached by two men, one showing a police badge and identifying himself as Charles Mackenzie, a lieutenant from the Winthrop, Massachusetts Police Department. Mackenzie would then recount a strange tale to the two young Coast Guardsmen.

Mackenzie informed them that his boat had caught fire earlier in the day and the motor was disabled. He and his friend had anchored the boat and then towed it to shore. Mackenzie asked Pratt to go and find his vessel and tow it in to Ipswich. There has been some speculation that the lieutenant may have been involved in some sort of nefarious activity, but this was never proven. The two Coast Guardsmen agreed and left the pier at about 9:15 p.m., heading out to Ipswich and toward Essex, where Mackenzie had told them he had anchored the boat. Little did Pratt and Faulkingham know that the disabled boat had already been discovered.

Base Seven in Gloucester was a busy Coast Guard installation in the late 1920s and 1930s, housing a surface operations unit and an aviation detachment. On August 4, 1930, the commander of Base Seven, E.A. Coffin, had departed on annual leave to New London, Connecticut, leaving the executive officer, Chief Boatswain Oscar Vinje, in charge.

In May 1929, Commander Coffin had written to Coast Guard headquarters, outlining, "What I thought were pertinent reasons for establishing a patrol in the Essex River, which was too shallow for our patrol and picket boats to operate in, and I requested for this duty authority to purchase an outboard motor boat of a certain type, and a motor for use with the boat."

The request was denied due to a lack of funding. A short while later, Commander Coffin purchased a small outboard hull using money from the canteen fund. He again wrote headquarters, this time informing them of the purchase and asking for funds to procure an outboard motor for the newly acquired hull. This request was allowed, and the boat was fully outfitted by the latter part of June 1930. The outboard was sixteen feet long, had a thirty-two-horsepower outboard and was painted gray with "U.S. Coast Guard Base Seven" painted in white letters on both sides of the hull.

On July 28, Commander Coffin's plan to "lie under the bank near the mouth of the [Essex] river, perfectly dark and quiet, and wait for anything to come in" was finally put into action. For five nights, starting on Monday, July 28, and continuing until Friday, August 1, three Coast Guardsmen went out to the river under the command of Warrant Officer (boatswain) John J. Olsen. Chief Motor Machinist's Mate Charles Palmquist and Chief Motor Machinist's Mate Hugh Olmstead were acting as crew.

These five nights were uneventful, and no patrol was scheduled for Saturday, August 2. Chief Palmquist took charge of the small boat on Sunday, August 3, and Chief Olmstead would take the Monday night patrol. He chose as his crewman Fireman First Class Clifford J. Hudder, who had only been in the service for eleven months. Chief Olmstead had no formal weapons training in the Coast Guard, only receiving training on the aircraft machine guns while in the Army Air Service. He had never been on a nighttime boarding or had charge of a Coast Guard small boat prior to leaving Base Seven on Monday, August 4. Clifford Hudder, twenty-one, had received less formal training and had never been trained in boarding boats. This was his first night patrol. Neither Chief Olmstead nor Fireman First Class Hudder had read or had been advised of the headquarters letter regarding Law Enforcement Circular of April 11, 1929.

A Fateful Day in Coast Guard History

Chief Olmstead and Hudder were issued a Lewis machine gun with two loaded pans of ammunition and one .45-caliber automatic pistol with five loaded clips. They left Base Seven between 6:30 and 7:00 p.m. They first stopped at Ten Pound Island off Gloucester to get a sweater for Hudder. Neither man was in uniform. Hudder was wearing dungaree pants, a sweater, a sheepskin jacket, black shoes and no hat. Chief Olmstead's "chief" cap was the only identifying article of clothing he was wearing.

Olmstead and Hudder then headed out of the Annisquam River and turned to port to head west to the entrance to the Essex River. Sunset on August 4, 1930, was listed at 8:00 p.m., and darkness began to fall on Ipswich Bay. Once at the mouth of the Essex River, Hudder reported seeing a vessel along the shore near Castle Neck. Hudder would later testify that Olmstead ordered him to display the ensign on the bow of the outboard boat. Olmstead "thought [this vessel] may have something to do with rum running."

The Coast Guard was assigned to stop smugglers during Prohibition, and here is the rumrunner *Mary*, *left*, after it was halted and brought to port. *U.S. Coast Guard photo.*

When they arrived on the scene, they found a white cabin cruiser with no one aboard. Once alongside, it was evident that there was fire smoldering in the engine room, and Olmstead jumped aboard and extinguished the fire using an old coat he found onboard. He also used some soaked canvas. After looking around the boat, he found "things were scattered around pretty much, the locker door was open, and it looked [to him] as though it had been left in a hurry."

Olmstead relayed his belief that this boat must be involved in rumrunning and told Hudder they would stay there for the night and wait to see if "the rummies" returned.

Soon, Hudder noticed a light off to seaward. They watched the area where he had seen the light, and soon the light flashed again. Olmstead told Hudder, "Here comes a rummy for sure." Olmstead would later recount that he told Hudder to "jump in our outboard and pull it alongside and hand me the machine gun because I thought it was a rummy." He instructed Hudder, "When I give the order, turn on the lights and put the search light on the Coast Guard ensign, and to fire warning shots, and to be sure to do it because things must be carried out quickly."

The other vessel was still approaching, and when Olmstead could make out the bow, he told Hudder to put the lights on and fire the warning shots. Hudder would later testify that he turned the running lights on and then trained the searchlight onto the ensign and fired seven warning shots. Hudder testified, "Almost at the same time Olmstead hollered at the other boat to come alongside, that we wanted to board it." He then recounted, "A short while after this, from the other boat, I heard someone holler, 'Give it to her' or 'Give it to them.'"

"I fired the machine gun at three different times. I just shot a few in it and waited to see if anything happened, and then shot a few more," Olmstead later recounted. He then had Hudder fire two illumination flames and saw the white vessel heading away from them. He tried to give chase to the outboard boat, but the engine wouldn't start.

All in all, seven rounds were fired from the .45-caliber pistol and twenty-nine rounds were fired from the Lewis machine gun. Twenty of the machine gun slugs would hit the hull of the Plum Island motor surfboat.

Meanwhile, Pratt and Faulkingham had left Ipswich Neck Wharf and safely navigated through the shifting shoals of the mouth of Plum Island Sound into open water. They turned to starboard once they were alongside the outer buoy and headed east toward the mouth of the Essex River. Approximately ten minutes later, Faulkingham noticed a dark object off the bow. He turned the tiller slightly and headed the motor surfboat toward the object, thinking that must be the vessel they had gone looking for.

Pratt was now up by the bow with a five-cell flashlight and was trying to illuminate the object. About eighty-five yards off the object, they could see now it was a boat. A light flashed on the boat. Faulkingham would later testify, "About that time we heard a shot and in a few moments a machine gun started."

Both men dropped down in the boat. Pratt said to Faulkingham, "We had better get away." It was obvious to Faulkingham that Pratt thought it was a rumrunner shooting at them. Faulkingham threw the tiller to starboard, and the motor lifeboat lumbered to port to try to evade the gunfire.

Faulkingham heard Pratt say, "I'm hit, are you?"

Faulkingham said, "Not yet."

Two flares were sent up from the area of the suspected rum boat. Faulkingham put the throttle to full and headed back in the direction of Ipswich Neck Wharf. Within forty-five minutes, they were at the wharf, and

The south end of Plum Island beach in Massachusetts looks much the same today as it did nearly a century ago during Prohibition. Smugglers would offload cases of liquor on the beach. *Dyke Hendrickson photo.*

Faulkingham enlisted the help of some local residents to get Pratt to the Cable Memorial Hospital in Ipswich.

Surfman Faulkingham took the motor lifeboat back to the Plum Island station to report the incident to the officer in charge. Faulkingham would later testify they never heard any shouts from the disabled vessel or heard any commands to "come alongside." He would also testify that neither he nor Pratt had yelled, "Give it to them."

Dr. O.F. Fountaine of Rowley was called at 10:30 p.m. When he arrived ten minutes later, he recalled that Pratt was suffering from "hemorrhage and shock, he was conscious and in his right mind." Dr. Fountaine testified that Pratt told him "he went out looking for a boat that had been adrift somewhere near Ipswich Beach." Dr. Fountaine also testified that Pratt had said, "Didn't have a chance, no warning at all, didn't have a chance."

Louis Pratt was still alive when his wife arrived at the hospital less than three hours after the shooting. He recognized his wife and asked if she had brought their daughter. Louis Pratt succumbed to his injuries shortly after, passing away in the early morning of August 5, 1930.

A Board of Inquiry found that Olmstead, chief motor machinist mate, be brought to trial by the general court on charges of violating a lawful regulation issued by the secretary of the treasury, to wit, "No person shall be negligent or careless in obeying orders or culpably inefficient in the performance of duty."

It was recommended that Chief Boatswain Oscar Vinje be reprimanded for not informing himself while temporarily in command of Base Seven of the plans and details of the patrol on the night of August 4.

Olmstead did stand court-martial, but a jury rendered a verdict of not guilty, stating that the serious charges had not been proven beyond a reasonable doubt. Vinje was cleared of wrongdoing.

The study by Considine and DuPont ended by saying, "Today's world and circumstances will thrust our Guardians into a very similar circumstance that Louis Pratt faced. As former Coast Guard Commandant, Adm. Thad Allen has summarized, 'All threats—All Hazards.' Louis Pratt encourages us to make sure we are truly, Semper Paratus—Always Ready."

Chapter 25

NEW ENGLAND'S
COAST GUARD CITIES

ROCKLAND, NEWBURYPORT, NEW LONDON

The Coast Guard has designated several communities in New England as Coast Guard cities: Rockland, Maine; Newburyport, Massachusetts; and New London, Connecticut. There are about twenty-five such cities throughout the country. A Coast Guard city is a U.S. municipality designated as such by the commandant of the Coast Guard on application of the local civilian government. It is an honorary designation intended to recognize communities of special importance to the Coast Guard. The program was created in 1998.

Applicants must meet criteria that can include erection of monuments and memorials to the Coast Guard, organization of civic celebrations on the anniversary of the founding of the U.S. Coast Guard, offer of special recognition and merchandise discounts to Coast Guard personnel by the local business community, providing support to local U.S. Coast Guard morale, welfare and recreation initiatives.

Designation as a Coast Guard city is for a five-year period but can be renewed indefinitely conditioned on the city continuing to meet the criteria.

ROCKLAND, CERTIFIED IN 2008

Rockland is a city of about seven thousand whose history has been marked by its proximity to water. It currently hosts a Coast Guard station with about thirty-three personnel. It maintains two vessels that can serve as icebreakers and buoy tenders. It also has several smaller rescue boats.

Indians called this place on the midcoast of Maine Catawamteak, or "great landing space." It produced lumber, lime and granite through the eighteenth and nineteenth centuries. Like in many coastal New England cities, shipbuilding became a dominant industry. By 1886, shipbuilding was surpassed by the lime business, which had twelve manufacturers employing one thousand workers. Fishing was also important.

The arrival of the railroad in 1871 brought an influx of tourists. Inns and hotels were established to accommodate them, with the grandest being the Bay Point Hotel in 1889. With a commanding view of the breakwater, the resort offered "every luxury and amusement." It was renamed the Samoset Hotel in 1902, and during the twentieth century, it hosted thousands of tourists who came for the view of Penobscot Bay or the golf that was on a

Coast Guard vessels tie up in Rockland. *Dyke Hendrickson photo.*

majestic course between the hotel and the water. The hotel burned down in 1969, but a new Samoset Resort opened in 1974.

The breakwater today is about seven-eighths of a mile long. Many think they will walk to the lighthouse at its terminus but find it is much longer than it looks. Most turn back.

Since the early 1990s, Rockland's economy has changed from a fishing community to a service center city. It has fostered a substantial increase in tourism, and the downtown has transformed into one of unique shops, boutiques, fine dining and art galleries.

It also hosts the well-appointed Maine Lighthouse Museum, which houses historic items from New England lighthouses. The facility also offers numerous historic photos and items related to the Coast Guard. It was pioneered by the late Coast Guard veteran Ken Black and his wife, Dot Black, who now runs the busy facility.

Rockland was named a Coast Guard city in March 2008, in recognition of the long-standing and special relationship that the city and its residents have with the service.

Newburyport, Certified in 2011

Newburyport is a small coastal and historic city about forty miles north of Boston. The population is about eighteen thousand, and it sits on the banks of the Merrimack River. A community with a vibrant tourism industry, Newburyport includes part of Plum Island. This is a barrier island about eleven miles long with memorable white sand beaches. The southern half of the island is occupied by the Parker River Wildlife Refuge, and its federal status means it has no houses or restaurants.

The mooring, winter storage and maintenance of recreational boats, motor and sail, still contribute a large part of the city's income. Close to 1,500 recreational vessels are registered in Newburyport each summer.

Newburyport is the birthplace of the Coast Guard. Although adherents of other Atlantic cities sometimes claim that title, a proclamation signed by President Lyndon Johnson in 1965 has settled that issue, at least for those in Newburyport. That document hangs on the wall of the Custom House Maritime Museum, a venerable stone structure built on Water Street in 1835.

The following is the story of how the Coast Guard was deemed to have started in Newburyport: In 1789, Secretary of the Treasury Alexander Hamilton told President George Washington there was very little money in the national coffers. Washington asked for suggestions on how to generate more. Hamilton, a native of the West Indies, knew much about ocean trade. He recommended that a revenue cutter service be created. He asked for funds to build ten cutters, which would travel along coastlines and harbors to discourage smuggling. The crew also would board vessels to ensure that captains were paying their customs taxes in full.

On August 4, 1790, Congress approved money for a Revenue Marine Service. Ten ships were built, and the first was launched in Newburyport in 1791. The vessel was the *Massachusetts*. It carried a crew of ten, with four officers, four enlisted men and two boys. It was armed with six small guns, but Hamilton entreated its captains to approach campaigns with tact and reason. By 1860, the organization was known as the U.S. Revenue Cutter Service. The modern Coast Guard was created in 1915 by the merger of the Revenue Cutter Service and the Life-Saving Service. The Lighthouse

City officials in Newburyport in recent years have built a riverside memorial and a harbormaster headquarters. *Dyke Hendrickson photo.*

Service was added in 1939. As one of the country's five armed services, the Coast Guard has been involved in every U.S. war from 1790 to the Iraq War and the War in Afghanistan.

Originally in Newburyport, at least one Coast Guard station was located on Plum Island, the barrier island connected to the mainland by a small bridge. In 1973, the Coast Guard station was moved into the city of Newburyport due to the challenges of erosion and difficulty of maintenance. Today, there are about two dozen people stationed there.

Newburyport is on the Merrimack River, a fast-flowing body of water that empties into the Atlantic. The entrance to the harbor is narrow, and sandbars form to make it unexpectedly shallow. The Coast Guard is often called to aid boaters who have run aground at low tide. Another reason they are called is that recreation vessels sometimes slam into the breakwalls through which the river runs into the sea. Station Merrimack River in Newburyport is one of just twenty stations designated as search-and-rescue posts because strong currents and high tide create a treacherous waterway.

Newburyport recognizes August 4 as the birthdate of the Coast Guard, with special activities during its weeklong Yankee Homecoming event. The local station offers tours of the facility and its forty-seven-foot rescue boats.

The Custom House Maritime Museum on Water Street is a major municipal asset and offers numerous exhibits focusing on the Coast Guard.

New London, Certified in 2017

New London is a seaport city located at the mouth of the Thames River in Connecticut. It was one of the world's three busiest whaling ports for several decades beginning in the early nineteenth century, along with Nantucket and New Bedford. The city subsequently became home to other shipping and manufacturing industries, but it has gradually lost most of its industrial base.

Numerous modern institutions continue to give it a nautical theme. It is home to the Coast Guard Academy and a Coast Guard station. The *Eagle*, the Coast Guard's tall ship, is homeported there.

The academy was built on the river in 1932. During World War II, the Merchant Marine Officers Training School was located at Fort Trumbull.

From 1950 to 1990, Fort Trumbull was the location for the Naval Underwater Sound Laboratory, which developed sonar and related systems

The Coast Guard Academy is a major institution in New London, Connecticut. *U.S. Coast Guard photo.*

for Navy submarines. In 1990, the Sound Laboratory was merged with the Naval Underwater Systems Center in Newport, Rhode Island, and the New London facility was closed in 1996.

The Navy Submarine Base New London is actually located in nearby Groton, but subs were stationed in New London from 1951 to 1991. In the 1990s, the State Pier was rebuilt as a container terminal. Numerous vessels catering to tourists use the pier to board vessels for whale-watching and party excursions.

Perhaps because of the city's commitment to the Coast Guard, alums and high-ranking officers are working to develop an elaborate Coast Guard Museum on the waterfront in New London.

Organizers are attempting to raise $100 million for the structure, which would be adjacent to the harbor and close to the downtown. Federal, state and municipal officials have made financial commitments, but in 2018, planners were striving mightily to raise money from the private sector.

The size and construction date have changed since the proposal was introduced. A recent version of the project suggested a five- or six-story, eighty-thousand-square-foot building that would include an outdoor concert pavilion where the famous U.S. Coast Guard Band and other groups can give concerts.

OTHER NAUTICAL CITIES

One cannot overlook the stature and influence of Boston. It serves as headquarters for the First Coast Guard District, which comprises New England, New York and northern New Jersey.

Headquarters is located in the North End of Boston and has been home to cutters including the *Escanaba*, the *Spencer*, the *Seneca*, the *Flying Fish* and the *Pendant*. The small boat station located on the base was reopened in 2003 after being closed in 1996.

Here is the way Coast Guard historians refer to Boston:

> *Sector Boston is a regional operational command responsible for coastal safety, security, and environmental protection from the New Hampshire–Massachusetts border southward to Plymouth, Massachusetts out to 200 miles offshore. Sector Boston directs over 1,500 Active Duty, Reserve, and Auxiliary members, four multi-mission response boat stations, four multi-mission cutters, and an Aids to Navigation Team to protect and secure vital infrastructure, rescue mariners in peril at sea, enforce federal law, maintain our navigable waterways, and respond to all hazards impacting the maritime transportation system and coastal region.*
>
> *The institutions that form the modern Coast Guard were born near here. The first commissioned cutter in the Revenue Cutter Service, the* Massachusetts, *was built in Newburyport in 1790, homeported in Boston, and commanded by Boston-born John Foster Williams; his final resting place is in the North End within sight of the Sector. Fabled lifesaver, Joshua James, served in the surfboat services from 1841 starting at age 15 until his death in 1902 at the age of 75; he was personally credited with over 200 lives saved. He received command of the Point Allerton Lifesaving Station in Hull, Massachusetts in 1889 at age 62 and died on the beach after drilling with his hand-rowed surf boat crew. During his 13-year command, his station was credited with 540 lives saved. The Coast Guard operates a station at Point Allerton to this day. Boston Light celebrated its 300th anniversary in September 2016 and was the first lighthouse constructed in what is now the United States.*
>
> *Built in 1716 on Little Brewster Island in Boston Harbor, it was destroyed by withdrawing British forces in 1776 during the Revolutionary War, and later reconstructed to the same exact dimensions in 1783 by the Massachusetts government. The Light was ceded to the United States government in 1790 and was administered under several lighthouse bureaus*

Members of the Coast Guard Auxiliary watch festivities in Boston Harbor. *U.S. Coast Guard photo.*

before being made part of the U.S. Coast Guard in 1939. It is the only remaining permanently manned lighthouse in federal service.

The men and women of Sector Boston maintain the same traditions as those who founded our nation and our service and serve the nation and coastal Massachusetts with the same dedication. We take inspiration from those that heroically laid our foundation and are devoted to remaining "Semper Paratus, Always Ready," just as they did.

Change of command ceremonies for top officers take place in historic Faneuil Hall in Boston.

On the subject of history, numerous coastal communities offer quality museums for Coasties and tourists alike. The Coast Guard Academy hosts a museum on its grounds, and admission is free. It contains memorabilia going back to the Revolutionary War. In downtown New London, the Custom House Maritime Museum offers a mix of history and entertainment. One of the city's noteworthy historic moments was in 1833, when the ship *Amistad* arrived in port with a vessel full of slaves who had taken control of the ship.

In modern times, Connecticut played a big role in developing helicopters for the Coast Guard. Some helicopters reached limited production in the

'30s, and in 1942, developer Igor Sikorsky of Stratford reached full-scale production with 131 aircraft built. Fast, large choppers with enormous lifting power have emerged as a valuable tool in the rescue of civilians on the Atlantic. Vintage Coast Guard choppers can be found in the New England Air Museum in Windsor Locks, Connecticut, at Bradley International Airport.

In Massachusetts, Barnstable hosts a Coast Guard museum with many displays that reference events that took place on Cape Cod and the islands. The museum's campus includes a blacksmith shop and one of America's oldest wooden jails (circa 1695). A mini theater offers films about local Coast Guard history. The easy-to-find facility tells the stories of predecessor organizations, including the U.S. Revenue Cutter Service, the U.S. Lighthouse Service and the U.S. Lifesaving Service, all of which have eighteenth-century roots in Massachusetts.

Gloucester has developed an excellent museum that melds fine art with the history of fishing. The Cape Ann Museum has an extensive collection of paintings of nineteenth-century artist Fitz Hugh Lane, also known as Fitz Henry Lane. The museum features a few Coast Guard displays. It was from Gloucester that many fishing vessels took to the sea, including the *Andrea Gail*. It was lost during bad weather, and the story of lost fishermen was told in the movie *The Perfect Storm*.

The Maine Maritime Museum in Bath, Maine, offers several displays focusing on the Coast Guard. This is a facility with enormous assets, including a twenty-acre campus and vessels that take out tourists in the summer.

STATIONS HAVE CLOSED BUT COAST GUARD IN NEW ENGLAND STAYS STRONG

C oast Guard actions that took place in New England have molded the national organization in several major ways.

It is the birthplace of the Coast Guard. In 1790, Secretary of the Treasury Alexander Hamilton prevailed on President George Washington to create a revenue cutter service. The first vessel, the *Massachusetts*, was built in Newburyport, Massachusetts. Largely for that reason, Newburyport is considered the birthplace of the Coast Guard. The anniversary date of the service is August 4, 1790.

Also, the development of the Humane Service and the Life-Saving Service have their roots in Massachusetts and other New England states. Both organizations were melded into the Coast Guard, which was formally named in 1915. The Lighthouse Service was merged into the service in 1939. If you live in New England, there is nothing more "New Englandie" than an oceanside lighthouse.

Another major development in the region was the birth of the modern helicopter, developed in Stratford, Connecticut. Inventor Igor Sikorsky worked for more than two decades to create a vehicle that could take off and land in a small area. He designed it to have the power to carry heavy loads. The Coast Guard was an early adopter of the helicopter. Choppers can rescue crews of recreational craft and commercial fishing vessels alike. It is a powerful weapon in the Coast Guard mission to save lives.

In addition, the Coast Guard Academy in New London was the first service academy to enroll women. This progressive decision is still playing

Coast Guard rear admiral Andrew J. Tiongson, commander, First Coast Guard District, based in Boston, speaks to service members during a security briefing. *U.S. Coast Guard photo by Petty Officer Third Class Steve Strohmaier.*

out, but it is clear that women—officers and enlisted personnel—have made great Coasties. The number of women is growing. In 2018, close to 40 percent of the entering class at the Academy were women. Females interviewed for this book said that the Coast Guard is an excellent career decision for women.

That said, the number of stations is diminishing. Today, there are more than two dozen Coast Guard active stations in New England. Many more outposts have closed with the development of maritime technology, including the introduction of choppers, powerful search-and-rescue vessels and up-to-the-nanosecond communications.

The following stations are active, according to Coast Guard records: in Maine, Boothbay Harbor, Kittery, Jonesport, Rockland, South Portland, Portland and Southwest Harbor; in New Hampshire, Portsmouth Harbor; in Vermont, Burlington; in Massachusetts, Boston, Bourne, Chatham, Gloucester, Nantucket, Newburyport, Hull, Provincetown, Scituate and Woods Hole; in Rhode Island, Block Island, Newport and Point Judith; and in Connecticut, New Haven and New London.

Many more stations have been closed. The following units in Maine are no longer active: Burnt Island (1891–1964); Cape Elizabeth (1887–1964); Cranberry Island (1880–1946); Cross Island (1874–1964); Crumple Island (1874–1952); Damariscove Island (1897–1960); Fletcher's Neck, Biddeford (1873–1955); Hunniwell's Beach, Phippsburg (1883–1971); Quoddy Head, Lubec (1873–1970); and White Head, St. George (1874–1956). The following units in New Hampshire are no longer active: Hampton Beach (1898–1969); Isle of Shoals (1910–54); Rye Beach (1874–1933); and Wallis Sands, Rye (1890–1938); The following units in Massachusetts are no longer active: Marshfield (1893–1953); Wellfleet (1873–1950); Dorchester Day, floating station (1896–1929); Coskata, Nantucket (1883–1953); Cuttyhunk (1895–1964); Fourth Cliff, Scituate (1879–1952); Duxbury (1878–1957); High Head, Truro (1882–1921); Truro, Highland (1882–1955); Madaket, Nantucket (1889–1956); Monomet (1874–1955); Aquinnah (1895–1955); Monomoy Island (1874–1955); Monomoy Point (1902–47); Muskeget (1892–1922); Nahant (1898–1963); Nauset, Eastham (1872–1948); New Bedford (closed 2003); Osterville (closed 1986); North Scituate (1884–1947); Chatham (1898–1947); Orleans (1873–1947); Truro, (1873–1938); Peaked Hill Bars, Provincetown (1872–1938); Plum Island, Newburyport (1889–1973); Salisbury Beach (1898–1939); Annisquam (1889–1964); Surfside, Nantucket (1874–1921); and Wood End, Provincetown (1896–1948). The following units in Rhode Island are no longer active: Brenton Point, Newport (1884–1946); South Kingston (1911–39); Narragansett (1887–1937); New Shoreham (1874–1937); Quonochontaug (1891–1939); Portsmouth (1898–1922); and Watch Hill (1879–1947).

Perhaps because they are covering more territory, Coasties in New England carry out more duties than ever. Most people do not know how many tasks there are and how much training goes into the development of an active member of the Coast Guard.

In the six New England states, the following missions include Aids to Navigation, Defense Readiness, Drug Interdiction, Ice Operations, Law Enforcement, Living Marine Resources, Marine Safety, Marine Environment Protection, Migrant Interdiction, Port and Waterway Security and Search and Rescue. Since this is an epilogue focusing on my two years traveling from northern Maine to southern New Hampshire to research this book, here are some parting thoughts on the missions.

Aids to Navigation: I toured the buoy tender *Juniper* in Newport and learned how valuable buoys, lighthouses, night lighting and satellite connections are to mariners of all stripes.

Defense Readiness: All veterans I met remembered exactly where they were during the terrorist attacks on September 11, 2001. The attitude of the Coast Guard altered overnight, and the prospect of violence became an everyday issue.

Drug Interdiction: I have a Facebook page that is not greatly patronized. But when I noted that the cutter *Escanaba* had returned from the Caribbean with six thousand pounds of illicit cocaine, I got nine hundred "likes" and about four hundred "shares." The comments were unanimous: people love the Coast Guard and the work it does.

Ice Operations: I was reminded that ice-breaking vessels travel up rivers including the Penobscot, the Kennebec and the Piscataqua during frigid winters. The vessels break up ice so that boats with heating oil for houses and businesses can make it upriver.

Law Enforcement: The Coast Guard aids many police actions in seeking to stop criminals whose actions include drug-running, theft and immigration violation. One intriguing story is in this book—the tale of a Coast Guard shootout with rum smugglers during Prohibition.

Living Marine Resource: Coast Guard vessels are charged with ensuring that commercial fishermen and recreational anglers do not break the law. The return of the striped bass in recent years is a direct result of regulation of the consumption of that fish. Commercial boats don't relish boarding by the Coast Guard, but they accept the requirement.

Marine Safety: Coast Guard vessels in recent years have been cracking down on excessive alcohol use on pleasure boats. Drinking on board must go back to Noah's Ark ("I'll take a pair of six-packs, not just one"). Still, the Coast Guard is stressing the importance of safety.

Marine Environment Protection: Coast Guard vessels react to events ranging from oil spills to excessive red tide.

Migrant Interdiction: Most officers of cutters that stop shiploads of migrants in the Caribbean say they are saving lives, not holding people back from coming to the United States. They say that most vessels are overcrowded and leaking. Without the Coast Guard's assistance, hundreds would drown when the unworthy vessels take on water.

Port and Waterway Security: I am impressed by how much work and training go into searching huge container vessels that enter New England ports. Trained Coasties try to search every possible hiding place as they look for weapons and/or drugs.

Search and Rescue: Almost to a man or woman, most said the major reason they joined was to save lives. Several added this sentiment: "To save lives without being shot at—or having to shoot someone else." Whatever the wording, most members are dedicated Americans who want to help those who take to the water.

BIBLIOGRAPHY

Beard, Tom. *The Coast Guard*. New York: Universe Publishing, 2016.

The Bulletin, the magazine of the Coast Guard Academy Alumni Association. New London, CT, August–September 2018.

Chernow, Ron. *Alexander Hamilton*. New York: Penguin Books, 2004.

Coast Guard. www.uscg.mil.

Custom House Maritime Museum. customhousemaritimemuseum.org.

Custom House Maritimes. Bulletin of Custom House Maritime Museum. New London, CT, 2018.

Evans, Stephen H. *The United States Coast Guard, 1790–1915*. Annapolis, MD: Naval Institute Press, 1949.

Facebook, numerous sites updated by individual stations.

Helvarg, David. *Rescue Warriors: U.S. Coast Guard, America's Forgotten Heroes*. New York: St. Martin's Griffin, 2010.

Hendrickson, Dyke. *Nautical Newburyport: A History of Captains, Clipper Ships and the Coast Guard*. Charleston, SC: The History Press, 2017.

King, Irving. *The Coast Guard Under Sail: The U.S. Revenue Cutter Service, 1789–1865*. Annapolis, MD: Naval Institute Press, 1989.

Korten, Tristam. *Into the Storm: Two Ships, a Deadly Hurricane and an Epic Battle for Survival*. New York: Penguin-Random House, 2018.

Kroll, C. Douglas. *A Coast Guardsman's History of the U.S. Coast Guard*. Annapolis, MD: Naval Institute Press, 2010.

Lochhaas, Tom. *Suddenly Overboard: True Stories of Sailors in Fatal Trouble*. New York: McGraw-Hill Education, 2013.

McCarthy, Tom. *The Greatest Coast Guard Stories Ever Told.* New York: Lyons Press, 2017.

Morison, Samuel Eliot. *The Maritime History of Massachusetts, 1783–1860.* Boston: Northeastern University Press, 1979.

Runion, Bria., *25 Awesome Facts about the Coast Guard: Odd and Interesting Truths about America's Most Forgotten Military Branch.* N.p.: Claw of Knowledge Publishing, LLC, 2015.

Salvatore, Joseph E., and Joan Berkey. *US Coast Guard Center at Cape May.* Charleston, SC: Arcadia Publishing, 2012.

Schreiner, Samuel A., Jr. *Mayday! Mayday!* New York: Donald I. Fine Inc., 1990.

Sea History magazine, National Maritime History Society, Peekskill, NY.

Shanks, Ralph, Wick York and Lisa Woo Shanks. *The U.S. Life-Saving Service: Heroes, Rescues and Architecture of the Early Coast Guard.* Novato, CA: Costano Books, 1996.

Slade, Rachel. *Into the Raging Sea: Thirty-Three Mariners, One Megastorm and the Sinking of El Faro.* New York: HarperCollins, 2018.

Smith, Bonnie Hurd, and Nelson Dionne. *U.S. Coast Guard Station Salem, Massachusetts: 1935–1970.* Salem, MA: Hurd-Smith Communications, 2015.

Thompson, Kalee. *Deadliest Sea: The Untold Story Behind the Greatest Rescue in Coast Guard History.* New York: HarperCollins, 2010.

Tougias, Michael J., and Casey Sherman. *The Finest Hours: The True Story of the U.S. Coast Guard's Most Daring Sea Rescue.* N.p., 2010.

Willoughby, Malcolm F. *Rum War at Sea.* Washington, D.C.: U.S. Printing Office, 1964.

ABOUT THE AUTHOR

Dyke Hendrickson is an author-journalist living in Newburyport, Massachusetts, birthplace of the Coast Guard. Several years ago, he wrote a multipart series for the *Daily News*, the local newspaper, on the history of that city. He realized that a concise overview of the maritime community had never been put in book form. Hendrickson then researched and wrote *Nautical Newburyport: A Story of Captains, Clipper Ships and the Coast Guard*, published by The History Press in 2017.

He is currently the outreach historian for the Custom House Maritime Museum in Newburyport. In that role, he speaks at schools, libraries and historical organizations to fulfill the museum's goal of taking history to the people. This is his fifth book. Hendrickson lives not far from the sea in Newburyport with his wife, Vicki Hendrickson. They have two children: Leslie, who lives in New York, and Drew, who is a resident of Somerville, Massachusetts.

Hendrickson is a graduate of Franklin and Marshall College with a degree in history, and he did graduate work at the University of Maine–Orono. He has been a writer and/or editor with the *Portland Press Herald*, the *New Orleans Times-Picayune* and the *Boston Herald*. Most recently, he was with the *Daily News* in Newburyport.

Visit us at
www.historypress.com